I READ YOU LOUD AND CLEAR ....SAY AGAIN?

Learning to hear the Controller's voice

GAYE MARTIN
(with **CONNIE NEUMANN**)

Copyright © 2014 Gaye Martin

All rights reserved. This book or any portion thereof may not be reproduced or used in any manner whatsoever without the express written permission of the publisher except for the use of brief quotations in a book review.

All Scripture quotations, unless otherwise specified, are from The Holy Bible, King James Version. Copyright © 1977, 1984, Thomas Nelson Inc., Publishers.

Scriptures marked NIV are from The Holy Bible, New International Version. Copyright © 1973, 1978, 1984 International Bible Society. Used by permission of Zondervan Publishing House. All rights reserved.

Scripture quotations marked TLB are taken from The Living Bible. Copyright © 1971 by Tyndale House Publishers, Wheaton, Illinois 60187. All rights reserved.

ISBN-13: 978-1-941733-15-8

Published by EA Books, Inc.
eabooksonline.com

Dedication

This book is dedicated
to my mother Frances Foster.
She was the first person
stationed on the runway of my life that
encouraged me to test my wings and to find
higher places to soar. She has never
wavered in her determination to call me not
only to my very best, but to find His very
best for my life. Mother, for sixty-two years of
prayers and support, and for showing me the
way into the Heavenlies, I thank you.
You are my hero.

"Once in a while you hear something that so powerfully speaks to where you are in your life that it becomes a part of you almost immediately. For a season you can remember the exact place where you were and the person used to deliver that truth to you, but often, that fades over time. I have tried valiantly to give credit for every illustration and bit of truth sown into my life by another, but if I have somehow overlooked anything or anyone, I beg your forgiveness. The omission was in no way intentional."

Table of Contents

Introduction

Part I - Static, Interference, Life...and Other Barriers to Listening

Chapter 1	You Can't Get Anywhere Without Leaving the Ground	3
Chapter 2	It's My Plane; I'll Fly It My Way	12
Chapter 3	Listening for My Call Letters	22
Chapter 4	I'll Tune to His Frequency—Right After This Song	29
Chapter 5	Must the Controller Have His Finger in *Every* Part of My Trip?	36
Chapter 6	When You're Cleared for Take-Off, It's Not Cool if You Don't Go Anywhere	48

Part II - Lifetime Enrollment in God's Flight School (or, Learning to Listen—Even When We Don't Want To)

Chapter 7	A Good Instructor Takes the Terror Out of Flying "Solo"	59
Chapter 8	From Controlled Crashes to Smooth Landings— Easier Said Than Done	68
Chapter 9	If You're Flying in Circles—Admit You're Lost	80
Chapter 10	When Visibility is Zero, Trust the One with the Whole Picture	89

Part III - Getting Our Wings—The Rewards of Listening

Chapter 11	Holding Patterns Are No Fun—But the Alternative is Worse	103
Chapter 12	Fly High; Pray Hard	111
Chapter 13	When He Says, "Climb and Maintain"—Hit the Throttle	121
Chapter 14	Clear New Pilots for Take-Off	130
Chapter 15	Are You a Real Pilot?	142

Introduction

> Pilot to Tower...Come in
> Tower...
> Is Anybody Listening?

Have you ever wondered if there really is a God? And if there is, whether He cares what happens to you?

The answer to both questions is a resounding YES! God does exist, and He is extremely interested in you as a person. The Bible tells us He keeps His eyes on even the smallest sparrow—and we are infinitely more important to Him.

The things that happen in our lives are not the result of fate, lady luck, or karma. Rather, our lives are guided by a loving Heavenly Father who always has our best interests in mind. As a pilot, I've realized that God's presence in our lives is much like an air traffic controller. We can't see the Controller, but we can talk to Him, and we know He is there looking out for our safety. He won't abandon us halfway to our destination or give us instructions meant to hurt us. But when His words fly in the face of our wishes or schedule, we often question, grumble, or complain. Thankfully, that does not cause Him to break out in a sweat. He does what is best for us—sometimes in spite of our groaning.

Learning to trust the unseen controller takes practice. More importantly, it takes faith and trust. It means crawling out on the runway and taking off for new horizons—even with knocking knees and chattering teeth.

But it is worth it. There is nothing in all the world like stepping out in faith with the Heavenly Controller, knowing He will guide you all the way. I won't kid you. The

Controller doesn't promise clear skies all the time. It will storm; it will sometimes get dark; but He will still be there to see you safely through.

Whether this is your first trip with the Controller, or whether you have been flying with Him for many years, this book is for you. A friend read the manuscript and said, "You can read it through quickly and chuckle; but then, when you are faced with a particular situation, you can go back to a certain chapter and gain deeper insight from it."

I pray these words will do more than make you smile. I pray they will encourage your heart.

                                              Gaye Martin
                                              Summerfield, Florida

Part I
Chapters One — Six

*Static, Interference, Life...
and Other Barriers to
Listening*

Gaye Martin

Chapter One

You Can't Get Anywhere Without Leaving the Ground

It was one of those cloudless Florida days where the sky stretches on forever. My friend and I were sitting in her Florida room, sipping coffee and watching the squirrels. I was comfortably relaxed—until she asked about my flight from Atlanta the day before.

"I was absolutely terrified," I confessed. "I was sure that plane was going to crash and I was going to meet Jesus."

I watched her eyes widen at the death-grip I had on my coffee mug. "Gaye, there wasn't a storm yesterday, was there?"

I shook my head, no.

"Thick clouds? Turbulence? Engine trouble?" No, no, no.

She didn't say anything, but I could *hear* what she was thinking. *How can a grown woman—the daughter of a pilot, no less—be that afraid of flying?* But I was. Every time I boarded a plane, it was a white-knuckle flight. Even today, it worries me that I board the plane from a "terminal."

Maybe your fears are different from mine. You may be afraid of closed places, of trying new things, or even of things in your past. Who among us hasn't been afraid at one time or another? I have fought fear all my life. Some of my fears are of things happening *again*; others are of things that *might* happen. I am afraid of horses because I was thrown once. I also live in fear that someone will discover my dress size. I don't mind if you know what I paid for it; I just don't want you to see what size it is.

But my greatest fear has been the fear of flying. My friend suggested that taking flying lessons might help. When I mustered up enough courage to actually get in the plane, I found that knowledge can indeed lessen fear. I not only got a pilot's license, but also discovered amazing parallels to my spiritual journey. I spent years spiritually parked because of my fear of new heights. I was as afraid to fly in my spiritual walk as I was of getting into an airplane. Isaiah 55:8-9 (NIV) finally helped me take to the skies. "For my thoughts are not your thoughts, neither are your ways my ways," declares the Lord. "As the heavens are higher than the earth, so are my ways higher than your ways."

That passage clearly calls us to reach for higher places in our relationship with the Lord. He wants us to soar to new heights with Him, but we can't do that without leaving our comfort zone. To know Him intimately you have to risk, and step out into the unknown. The problem is not the fear itself; the problem is that we let the fear paralyze us. Because He has promised to be with us always, we can take off—in the face of our fears.

Several years after I got my pilot's license, my family accompanied me to Atlanta for a week of meetings. On the return trip, we were cleared all the way to our destination in Florida with no problems in sight. It was a cold winter day and we were having a great time together—for the first 20 minutes. Then we got into freezing rain, a pilot's nightmare. Buildup of ice on the windshield destroys visibility, and ice on the wings tampers with airflow—which is technical lingo for "you can crash."

That was not an option on my agenda, so I contacted the tower in Atlanta and told them my problem. They suggested I climb to a higher altitude to see if I could get out of the storm. I climbed, but I was still in it. They suggested I try descending; nothing but more ice buildup on wings and windshield.

At that point, I knew we were in real trouble, and my family knew we were in real trouble. My children didn't fuss over who would pray that day; they all prayed. They all prayed more than once. Finally the controller said, "You have no choice but to look for a flat field and put her down while you still have a bit of visibility." I wished I could do something simpler—like perform major surgery.

I searched the ground for a place to land safely. Sure enough, there was a field long enough to land in and isolated enough not to endanger those on the ground. I prayed as I lined up with that field, and prayed some more as I looked for the right place to touch down. The clouds shifted just a bit—and I did a double take. Right next to that field was a runway.

I landed at Hazelhurst, Georgia, without a clue as to where I was. We had to wait three days for the weather to clear, though I did consider waiting for the spring thaw. My children opted to take a bus home, but that's okay. One day circumstances will leap into their lives and they will have to lean on the heavenly Controller's advice to get them through safely. They will learn what I have learned: He will get them through. He always does.

You Gotta Start Somewhere

But whether in a plane, or in your spiritual walk, you can only sit on the end of the runway for so long. I have often been in the cockpit of my little plane, waiting for clearance, and when it comes, I'm not sure this is really what I want to do. You can only hold up other traffic so long before the controller asks you to "declare your intentions." That's aviation lingo for "move, or get off the runway." There were times in my life I have had to declare my intentions. Even our Father will sometimes set us on the sidelines until we are prepared to commit.

I often deal with this fear of getting started in the area of weight loss. I can't tell you how many diet programs I planned for in the hanger, revved up my engines to start, and then did nothing but sit on the end of the runway. Recently, I taxied out for a fresh go at it after I went walking one morning. I try to walk two miles every day, which is my stab at cardiovascular health. Of course, I also reward myself with a donut when I get back home. A retired gentleman lives a few streets over from me, and the extent of our conversation when we pass each other about 6:30 every morning goes something like this:

"Morning."

"Morning."

"Think it's going to rain?"

"Hope not."

"Hope you get home before it does."

"Uh, huh. Me too."

One day last year after we'd said the usual things, he said, "You certainly are consistent at that."

"Yes, sir, I am."

"How long have you been at it this time?"

"About 9 months."

He said, "Well, it's not working."

I wanted to call out, "I hope a truck runs over you today," but I didn't. The motivation of that morning put me on the runway of my local health spa. Aside from the obvious, the reason I did is because I was tired of Sea World calling and wanting to know how I look in black and white—and if I do hoops. I said, "I look great in black and white, and I can learn hoops. But I refuse to give birth in the pool, cause I don't think that's cool." So I joined the local health spa. (Incidentally, I am thinking of giving my lifetime membership away as a reward to someone who purchases this book. You have to be lucky to get it, but not real lucky.)

The first time I went to the spa, I immediately realized my body was not going to impress the cute little girl who checked me in. I decided to impress her with my mind. She gave me a questionnaire to fill out, and on the blank line next to the word "weight" I put down, "None of your business. God does not know." The reason I know He doesn't, is because I've never told him. And He wouldn't peek at the scale, I just know He wouldn't.

The next question said, "goal," so I put down "Significant reduction of surplus adipose tissue." I handed the form back to Miss Perky and she said, "Umm...lady, this is not a clinic." I guess she thought, that I thought, we were going to do liposuction in the back. Which I could have handled, because I tried that once with the vacuum cleaner, but all you get is hickeys. Do you know how bad you look when you do that on your chin?

I joined the spa, and I joined Miss Perky's aerobics class. During my first class, I noticed she had a rosebud tattooed on her thigh. I went home and said to my husband, Phil, "I hope we don't have to do that to belong to this class." Thank goodness we didn't, because if I had tattooed a rosebud to my thigh at that time, it would be in full bloom today!

One way the Lord remedies our delays on the runways of life is by encouraging us to "count the cost." In Luke 14:28 (NIV) Jesus told his disciples, "Suppose one of you want to build a tower. Will he not first sit down and estimate the cost to see if he has enough money to complete it?" Most of us impulsively don't calculate the full investment of the plans we make, or we taxi out in an early commitment that leaves us frustrated when we can't find the energy, strength, or true motivation to make the trip. I have to say I learned not to press others or myself for a quick commitment. If you need an immediate answer to a proposal, then I have to say, "No I can't. I must have time to run it by the Controller and wait on His clearance."

Other times, people tell me they have counted the cost, and want to step out for the Lord, but are afraid they lack knowledge. They don't know the Bible well enough, they say, or they haven't been to Bible school. While flying, I learned that you can have a temporary lapse in memory over the correct procedure or proper direction in which to fly. But if you are well trained, that training will kick in and deliver the insight or wisdom you need to successfully resolve the issue. The same principle is true of the Word. The enemy of our soul would have us neglect God's "manual" because we don't understand every word, or can't seem to memorize it and quote it verbatim. I promise you—and God promises you—that if you read it and hide it in your heart, when you need it the Holy Spirit will call it up. He will present it to your mind and heart to help you resolve the situation. John 14:26 tells us, "He will teach us all things and bring all things to our remembrance." Don't let the enemy keep you from stepping out in faith.

Courage is not being without fear. Courage is taking a step forward in spite of the fear. I have had to do that when an engine in the plane ran rough—or quit altogether when I changed from one fuel tank to another. It sure gets quiet right before you start to scream. I wanted to scream the day I landed in Hazlehurst, Georgia. Instead, I prayed for guidance and told my family "Don't worry, everything will be fine."

My granddaughter, Stephanie, called me one morning at 5:00 a.m.

"Nanie, do you have time to talk?"

Talk? At 5:00 a.m.? "Sure, Sugar, what do you need?" I asked.

She hesitated, then said, "I'm home alone. Mom took my brother to his field trip."

Naturally, my next question was, "And why did you not go with her?"

"Because," she continued, "I was just trying to prove I'm brave. Can you talk till she gets home?"

I've done that—oh, how many times I have done that—just trying to prove I'm brave.

Face Fear at a Dead Run

Sometimes you simply have to face your fears and conquer them. There is just no other way. When our five children were young, we bought them a horse. You know how parents are, we want our children to have all those things we didn't have, so we bought a horse. We would go out to the farm, and Fran would ride Candy while I sat on the fence. One day Fran said, "Mother, I want you to ride her."

I said, "No, I want to remember me sitting on the fence, and you on the horse." She did finally talk me into riding because she wanted to define her own little memory there, and I was afraid I was going to mess up her psyche, so I got on the horse. I should not have done that, because that horse threw me. But before she finally got rid of me, she took me pell-mell down country roads, over hedges, and under carports.

Some years later, Phil and I went out to Yellowstone Park. I said, "You know, it is really time I faced my fears. Tell you what, I want you to buy tickets for the trail ride tomorrow." I figured that was safe, because you don't ever hear of anybody dying on the trail ride.

"Are you sure?"

"Absolutely. Absolutely." So he bought tickets for the trail ride.

When I got up the next morning, I was so upset, I was sick to my stomach. Child, you need to know it was awful. Phil was thrilled about going, because he loves to ride. I said, "I don't know if I want to do this."

But I did get up on the horse, and the best part of my story is that I was astride something with bigger hips than I have. That horse moved just a little bit, and I was terrified. It played old tapes of when I'd been thrown.

I sent a look to Phil that only a wife can send a husband. It said, "Please. I have to get off this horse."

Phil sent a look back that only a husband can send a wife. It said, "We paid eight bucks for these tickets. You're going to ride."

Our trail guide—a lady who looked like she'd been born on a horse—said, "I'm going to call you by your horses' name because I don't know any of you, and I'm only going to be with you a couple of hours. Just ride in trail as I call your horse's name." She was calling out names like Gunsmoke, and Bullet, and I was back there praying I was on Fluffy. You know who I was on? Lightning.

I came home with a migraine headache you wouldn't believe. The tickets for the trail ride cost Phil sixteen dollars, but my visit to the emergency room that night cost him a whole lot more. But I do believe I've conquered my fear. I figure if I sat on the horse, I conquered the fear. And I sat on the horse.

That's courage. The enemy tells us if there is any fear, you have no courage. Wrong. The phrase Jesus used the most was "Fear not." He is well aware of our fear. He said "I will never leave you or forsake you. So we may boldly say, The Lord is my helper and I will not fear what man shall do unto me" Hebrews 13:5-6.

I have learned I can follow the Controller's voice anywhere; I can trust His voice through anything. I can rest in the knowledge that He knows where I am even when I don't. I know that when things have spun out of my control, they have not spun out of his. I know that His arm is not short and His eye is not blind. He will show himself strong on behalf of his children.

Ohhh, move over fear, I feel courage.

Chapter Two

It's My Plane,
I'll Fly It My Way

Once I got past my initial terror, I was surprised to realize I enjoyed my flying lessons. Even though I felt I had conquered the fear—at least some it—I welcomed my instructor's presence in the next seat. He represented knowledge, experience and a strong blanket of security. It's cozy in the cockpit when you are with someone who can oversee the flight.

But after weeks of flying together, listening to his repeated advice, warnings and instructions, I felt more than saturated with information and quite capable. "I know, I know," I said. "Preflight the airplane, file a flight plan, use the check-list, don't depend on your memory. Gotcha!"

Then came the day I thought long overdue. I had the routine down pat, so I let my mind wander a bit and approached the runway thinking, *Do I have time to stop by the mall on my way home?*

As we taxied the instructor suddenly said, "Let me out here and take it once around the airport by yourself."

"Excuse me? Uh...now? Today? " *Before I go to the mall?* It's a heart stopper—even when you think you're prepared.

I taxied down the runway, took off and flew once around the landing pattern, and then touched down again. I never actually lost sight of the airport, but a million things ran through my mind. *Can I get it in the air? Can I get it down? What's that noise? I've never heard that noise before. Where is the fuel gauge? Where is the seat belt? Where is the parachute? WHERE IS MY MOTHER?*

Not until I rolled back up to my instructor did I take my thumb out of my mouth and give him a wet thumbs up.

"How did you do?" my instructor asked.

"Great."

"Any problems?"

"None."

"Any questions?"

"Yes, where is the bathroom?"

Not long after that my instructor said, "When can you do your solo cross-country?" Now the theme song humming in my heart since I was about six years old has been, "I can't wait to do it my way!" The thought of cutting the umbilical cord to my flight instructor tapped its toe to my song. SOLO means I am on my own. SOLO means I am in control. SOLO CROSS-COUNTRY means I'm on my own and in control for a long time. Good-bye, Florida. Hello, Texas.

However, you don't just get in the plane and take off. For your cross-country, the instructor assigns you a city to fly to. You must land at that city, get your log book signed—so they know you didn't take Greyhound—and return to the point of origin. My assigned cross-country was from Miami to Stuart, approximately 200 miles. I wasn't too worried, because flying in Florida is not all that difficult. You can get almost anyplace if you fly low enough to read the signs on I-95.

I remember that morning so well. I calculated my time of departure, factored in the winds and came to a fairly decent ETA (estimated time of arrival) to Stuart. I also remembered to file my flight plan, so if I crashed and burned they would know where to look. The only detail undone was actually getting into the airplane and taking off. When I did, I flew just as close to the ground and I-95 as I could.

I finally lined up on the runway at Stuart, landed and got out of the plane. Next I had to go into the terminal and ask them to sign my log book to document that I came by plane, not car. Now you don't want to look green when you go in there, but the fact is, you are green. My little log book still smelled like a new magazine. I squared my shoulders and approached the desk, where they greeted me with "Welcome to West Palm Beach."

Oh, no, what do I do now? Do I act like I wanted to go to West Palm Beach? Or do I laugh hoping this is a sick joke? I laughed. They laughed. Another new pilot initiated into solo flight.

It's an illusion to believe that any part of our life is a solo flight. Life is a team sport and our success at it depends largely on how we relate to the other players on the team. Looked at more closely, even our Salvation extends beyond merely a decision *for* Christ to a relationship *with* Christ. The whole purpose of God's dealing with man from the beginning is that He might "dwell among them" (Exodus 25:8). That sounds like a relationship to me.

Humanity's response to God's leading seems to follow a similar pattern. At first, we welcome His presence into our fractured and shattered lives. He comes with hope, answers, and a mantle of security. However, after learning and accepting instruction from Him for a season, we are prone to feel rather saturated and capable within ourselves. Enough so that Paul gave the Galatians a stern reproof.

> O foolish Galatians, who hath bewitched you, that ye should not obey the truth, before whose eyes Jesus Christ hath been evidently set forth, crucified among you? This only would I learn of you,

Received ye the Spirit by the works of the law, or by the hearing of faith? Are ye so foolish? having begun in the Spirit, are ye now made perfect by the flesh? Have ye suffered so many things in vain? if it be yet in vain (Galatians 3:1-4).

The day my instructor got out of the plane to test my skill, he never left the runway. At a time when I was so sure I could now begin to handle it by myself, I was under the ever-watchful eye of the one teaching me to fly. In fact, for years he has governed my trips with the instructions he invested in me years ago. In the same way, my heavenly Father deposits His Word in my heart, and I can hear His voice surface in every facet of my journey.

He also sends people to guide us. The first person posted on the runway of my life was my mother. Her watchful eye and praying heart signaled her concern and encouragement every time I tried my wings in a new direction.

"Must You Pray in My Room?"

I was raised in a praying home. I haven't always been proud of that, but I am extremely proud of it today. One of the earliest recollections I have of my mother is waking up in the middle of the night and finding her praying for me at the foot of my bed. Now that irritated me no end. First, that she thought I needed it worse than my brother, and second that she had chosen my bed to pray beside rather than her own.

Almost every evening was punctuated with a Bible story where she dramatically read each part. I am sure she often felt these stories were forever lost on us as they only briefly replaced our requests for more of "The Little Engine that Could" and other in-depth, exciting stories. It is only now that I realize the stories she carefully chose and the prayers she boldly prayed were all part of a deal she had struck with God when she was a young woman. She gave me to God before He gave me to her. Even the most independent of souls can't fight a praying Mother who is in partnership with God. What all this did was equip me with quiet confidence and a seductively rising set of values scattered like yeast over my mind and heart.

Dad's Lesson in Decorum

I never questioned my parent's value system—well *almost* never questioned their value system. Come to think of it, by about age 13, I had questioned every part of it and eventually rejected it altogether. To demonstrate my vast maturity at this point, I remember an incident I'm sure my father has fervently prayed to forget. Those were the wonderful days of drive-in restaurants, with curb service and car hops. My aspirations soared to think I might someday hold that coveted position at the very popular drive-in in town called "The Big Wheel." Could life offer more than to wear white shorts with white tasseled boots and to walk up to the county's finest and say "What kin I get fer ya? Tonight's Big Wheel Deal is..."

Oh, heady thoughts of great opportunity. In the meantime, I researched that lofty position with various dates as we ended an evening at the Big Wheel.

On one occasion my father cautioned me not to "socialize" on the periphery of the Big Wheel's parking lot, but rather, my date and I should enjoy our meal in the immediate vicinity of the restaurant. His reasoning went something like this: he was the Training Director for a major airline and we had a reputation to uphold—primarily his. I was expected to make a contribution to this reputation by my conduct. His request seemed a bit selfish to me and I decided at the next opportunity to see what "forbidden fruit" I was sacrificing for his reputation.

I had no sooner agreed with my date that we should find a quiet corner and perched myself under his arm, when I heard a tap on my window. It was not the much-envied car hop, there to take our order. It was my father, and as I rolled down the window I blurted out, "You don't trust me."

I will never forget his face as he bodily transferred me from one car to another. I wondered if I'd ever see the Big Wheel again, not to mention my hoped-for career there. He had just ruined my life, my whole life. I never did become the illustrious car hop.

Unfortunately, I reacted to the rules of flying much as I had to my father's. There were so many rules and restrictions that *corseted* even an afternoon of floating above it all. It seemed each one was designed to cinch away the coveted freedom that drove me to the airport initially. I questioned every rule and the wisdom of it. Though I could imagine that "someone" somewhere might fly into a situation where they would need them, I couldn't envision myself ever being there. I bent the rules regularly. Even broke some small ones. I learned you can break a small rule and end up with a BIG mistake. Students ask me from time to time "How did you learn that?" My answer is always, "Through mistakes." Mistakes with a little time tacked on become wisdom.

Is This All There Is?

Because I found the rules in our home so restrictive—after all, the night before I got married I had to be in at nine p.m.—I rationalized that of course I must attempt to accomplish between seven and nine what "everyone else" was doing between nine and eleven. I decided on the basis of these restrictions to marry and leave home and do what young people today call "doing your own thing, steering your ship, in charge of my destiny." As far as I can see, in my case all of that could have been summed up in one bumper sticker: pre-pubescent at the wheel. Which is, of course, against the law. It is safe to say I was better acquainted with the driver's handbook than I was with the marriage manual when I took the plunge into matrimony. My primary concern through the entire process was a blemish-free face for the ceremony. That was not to be, which may have been prophetic for the problems that union would face in the future.

I began married life with the same dedication I had given to the courtship and the planning of the ceremony. If I didn't feel like cleaning the house, I didn't clean the house. If the Board of Health had seen it, they would have condemned it.

A year later we began our family. I was six months pregnant when it dawned on me, *I'm not cut out to be a mother*. That is a TERRIBLE time to find out you're not cut out to be a Mother. I had a growing vacuum and vacancy in my life—that no one and nothing could fill. Marriage was not fulfilling, going to work was not fulfilling, my hobbies were not fulfilling, and here was motherhood on the horizon and THAT prospect was not fulfilling. I didn't know if my problem was physical or emotional. I KNEW it wasn't spiritual since my mom had taken care of that when I was little. I remember at the ripe old age of 17 saying to my doctor, "Is this all there is to life? The only two things I haven't done yet is go through menopause and die, and I don't want to do either one."

Mom to the Rescue

It was during this time my mother came to the rescue. You know how when children begin to come along, you realize what a neat Mom you have? I now have children who are married with families who know what a wonderful Mom I am. However, I have one son who is not married and does not yet know my worth. I am not worried; marriage and children will bring all that into focus for him.

One panic-filled morning mother called and asked if I'd like to go out that evening. "Oh mother, I need a night out so bad. Where are we going?"

"Church."

Even though I cut my teeth on a pew, I hadn't been to church in ages. I knew that had hurt my mother, so I decided it would be *very good* for my mother if I went to church with her.

That night I attended a little church I've never been in before or since. In that church, I met Jesus Christ face to face and my Mother's God became my God. I have never been able to say I found Him, because I didn't. I wasn't even looking for Him. However, I now know He had been looking for me. He had been looking for me through the prayers of my Mother and Father—which I considered an invasion of my privacy. He had looked for me through neighbors who had invited me to local churches—which I also saw as an invasion of my privacy. He had even looked for me through invitations to Christian organizations — which offended me at the time. How I resisted Him and fought His search for me.

Three Scriptures were read that night that forever changed my life and I'd like to share them with you. The first one is found in Luke 19:10, "For the Son of Man is come to seek and to save that which was lost." Now that was terminology I didn't altogether understand. I didn't know what lost meant, but it sounded like I felt: no roots, no security, and no sense of direction. I didn't know what saved meant, either, but it sounded like I wanted to feel. It sounded like a rescue of sorts.

The second scripture is in Romans 10:9, "That if thou shalt confess with thy mouth the Lord Jesus, and shalt believe in thine heart that God hath raised him from the dead, thou shalt be saved." Well, that seemed easy enough to do.

The third scripture had its greatest impact on me and is found in 2 Corinthians 5:17, "Therefore, if any man be in Christ, he is a new creature: old things are passed away; behold all things become new." That means relationships, attitudes, reactions, and even finances. So on the basis of those scriptures, I prayed a very simple prayer.

"Jesus, as a result of what I've heard here tonight, I'm willing to entertain the thought that my need might be a spiritual need. I understand you have made me a creature of free will and will not violate that in any way without a personal invitation from me. If that is the case, I personally invite you to come into my life and take control. Will you do for me what I have been unable to do for myself? Forgive me for those things I've done that were displeasing in your sight, that which you call sin. I repent of them. Thank you, Amen."

God Respects Our Free Will

If you have never asked Jesus to come into your life, I invite you to do that. Right now, wherever you are. God loves you and wants the very best for your life—and He wants you to spend eternity with Him. But He will not force His way into your life. He comes only by personal invitation from you. Ask Him. He will fill the emptiness and give your life meaning.

If you have already asked Him into your life, is He in control? Do you submit your plans and decisions to the Heavenly "air traffic Controller" for His approval and input? Or do you go through life saying, "It's my plane; I'll fly it my way!"

Besides speaking to us in a still, small voice and through His word, God also posts people on the runway of our lives; encouraging, warning, and directing. But the final decision is ours. The success or failure of our journey depends on how we process instruction and the choices we make in light of it.

Are you flying "my way" or God's way?

Chapter Three

Listening for My Call Letters

I hate delays, don't you? If I drink Slimfast, I expect to lose 30 lbs. that afternoon. I expect my toenail polish to dry instantly, and if I order a cheeseburger at a fast food restaurant, I expect it to be flying out the window when I drive up.

I especially hate runway delays. They make me wonder if the controller forgot me—or I missed hearing my call letters. Numerous times I contacted the tower for take-off clearance, only to be told to wait on the taxiway. I had many quietly muttered arguments with ground control. "Excuse me, is anyone there?...Are you on coffee break?...Is it your deal? Who won the last hand?...I would like to go before the elastic wears out on my pantyhose."

One day in Jacksonville, Florida, my passengers and I were waiting on the assigned taxiway while larger aircraft were cleared for take-off. I know my voice betrayed my annoyance more than once that day. "Goodnight," I mumbled, "what do I have to do to get some service?"

Finally, the controller gave in and cleared me for a hasty take-off just as a commercial jet climbed into the sky ahead of me. I thanked him and taxied quickly onto the runway. *At last*, I thought as I gave it power and began to roll out.

Suddenly, our plane was picked up and slung into the grass some 50 feet away. What force!! I meekly crept back out onto the runway, re-applied for take-off clearance, and took off without further incident.

I later learned that demon wind was the result of turbulence from the departing jet. That explains why the controller often holds smaller aircraft aside until larger ones are cleared. He knows the effects large jets will have long after they take off. I am sure the Jacksonville controller decided a little dose of experience would do wonders for my impatience. It did. Not only did I have three passengers feel called into full-time Christian service, but I will also wait a week to take off after a jet. In fact, I will shave my legs and floss my teeth if I can work it in.

In Psalm 139:17-18 we are reminded that we are never out of our father's thoughts. "How precious it is, Lord, to realize that you are thinking about me constantly. I can't even count how many times a day your thoughts turn towards me. And when I waken in the morning, you are still thinking of me" (TLB).

"Pass It On Lady"

I learned early on how often I am in His thoughts, beginning with a little lady who spoke to me the night I accepted Christ as my Savior. She said, "First, tomorrow you are going to think what happened tonight was just an emotional experience." She was right, I did. "But don't believe that for a minute. Second," she continued, "if you want to know absolutely and positively for sure that Jesus is real, from now on, when you have a need, tell it to no one but to Him."

I didn't exactly know what she meant, but two months later I received a forty-six dollar bill from Florida Power and Light. I had received this bill more than once. In fact, this one arrived on Monday and informed me that if the bill was not paid by Tuesday, they were going to terminate service.

Those were the days when we could not afford a checking account. We were married ten years before we had a checking account. I am sure some of you remember those days. For those of you who don't know, if you didn't have a checking account, you had envelopes. Every week I would cash my husband's check, put two dollars behind insurance, and fifteen dollars behind groceries. Remember when fifteen dollars or less bought a week's worth of groceries? And do you remember what we called it when a crisis arose and we would fly through all the envelopes to find enough cash to solve it? Robbing Peter to pay Paul.

I flew through all my envelopes, and I didn't have forty-six dollars. My parents were out of the country, so I couldn't borrow it from them. Household Finance had told us not to come back until we had paid up. If you have ever borrowed from Household Finance, you know that's your first thirty-year loan. It's awful; you don't ever get them paid off.

We didn't have forty-six dollars.

Then I remembered what that lady told me. I didn't know how to pray, so I just went into my bedroom and said, "Jesus, I don't know if this constitutes a need or not, but I need forty-six dollars." I told Him exactly how much I needed, in case He's super-busy. There are people who will tell you God is so busy taking care of Big things, like world peace, that He can't be bothered with little things. What those people don't know is this: that was big to me that day. To be honest, it eclipsed world peace in my mind. I said, "Jesus I need it, and I need it by tomorrow. Thank you. Amen."

Something happened the next day that had never happened to me before. In the mail, I received a forty-six dollar money order from a man I'd never met. Attached to the money order was a little scrap of brown paper bag that read, "God told me to send you this. A friend in Christ."

Is God real? Well, I guess.

I could hardly wait on my phone bill to come in.

That money order came from the manager of a 7-Eleven I had never been in. It took me months to find him, and months to try to pay him back, but he wouldn't take it. "You're not supposed to pay it back," he said.

"Well, what are you supposed to do?"

"Lady, you're supposed to pass it on." I have tried to do that.

Blessings—and Shoes—by the Dozen

Besides not being able to afford a checking account, those were also the days when you only had two pairs of shoes. Remember those days? You had a Sunday pair and an everyday pair. My Sunday pair happened to be in pretty bad shape. It wasn't that I didn't have the money to buy a new pair, but you know how it is when the kids are coming up; you don't feel you can spend money on yourself.

I'm over that now. These days I spend it before they know we have it. I say, "Happy Tuesday to me. Happy Wednesday to me." A few times I've spent it before Phil knew we had it, and then said, "Do you want to see what you bought me today?"

But back then I was afraid to spend it on myself, so I said to the Lord, "Jesus, if you could see your way clear, I need a pair of Sunday shoes. Thank you. Amen." I checked the mail every day. Isn't it funny how we get the idea that if God moved one way one time, He's locked into moving that way every time? I don't think so. God is far more versatile than that.

The next time I attended the home Bible study I belonged to, the lady of the house said, "Can you stay after everyone leaves?"

Later she said, "Gaye, I hope you're going to understand what I'm going to tell you. You've been on my heart so much lately, that I did something yesterday I hope you're going to understand."

Now I was really curious. "What did you do?"

"I went to the 163rd Street Shopping Center in North Miami and bought you seven pairs of shoes."

I tell you those two stories to illustrate a point: when you invite Him to come into your life, He begins to meet the needs you have at that time. Back then, my needs were material needs. Things are much better now. We have our Thanksgiving turkey on layaway, and we only owe two more payments. I must tell you He's done much more than meet my material needs. He has taught me to listen for His instructions—even when there is static and noise all around.

As a new pilot, my most significant problem was not following instructions, but *hearing* them. You must train your ear to hear beyond the static to decipher what kind of clearance or hold the controller has issued you. In the beginning I had to have complete silence in the cockpit as I listened for his voice. "Shhh, quiet," as I strained to hear. *Are those my call letters? Were the instructions for me or the American Airlines jet?* Keep in mind, the controller is usually talking to more than one pilot; issuing instructions, and clearing planes for take-off or landing. Take it from someone who knows, when he clears a commercial jet for take-off, it is not cool for you in your little plane to go leaping out onto the runway.

How often do we also have a simplistic idea of what it means when He calls us into a higher walk? I spent years thinking, *Righteousness? I can do that. I'll need a week or so, but it's no big deal.* Two days later I would discover I need instruction, and a lot of it. It has not been easy to learn to hear my heavenly Father's voice over all the static and interference we encounter today. Believe me, it is easy to get signals crossed and think the instructions for another are also for you.

We have friends who are missionaries to Albania. Every time they come home, they stay with us for a few days and tell us all the miraculous ways God is speaking to them and leading them. Pretty soon I feel called to Albania. But after a few days—usually before I apply for a passport—I realize that I once again tried to apply someone else's set of instructions to my life.

The Home Sherman Spared

There are other times, though, when His voice is so clear, there is no mistaking it. One cold winter night an insistent noise woke me. I jumped out of bed and raced into the living room. Everything looked normal, but that screeching sound was not. Then it dawned on me, *Oh, it's just the new smoke alarm...Wait a minute, smoke alarm?!*

Fear grew fur and fangs and jumped up in my face. Not again, not again. Years earlier I had lost a home to fire, so the fear was never far away. I went from room to room in a panic, searching for the heat. I felt every wall, certain the fire was somewhere in the crawl spaces with the squirrels. Remembering how quickly the last house was consumed, I rushed back to the bedroom, threw our valuables in the center of the bed and called Phil at work. "Hurry home, the house is on fire."

I snatched the bedspread up around the pile of possessions and drug it out into the front yard. Then I went back in and got the children and animals. (I know, I know.)

About the time Phil arrived, we were all shivering in the yard, trying to determine where the flames would erupt. I looked at the house and thought back to when we bought it. I loved it on sight. The hardwood floors had paths of history carved into them, and the house had long ago settled with a definite slope to the South. You didn't notice it until you spilled milk on the floor. Then you had to run after it to wipe it up before it ran under the refrigerator. Each of us had formed rather strong ties to our little "turn-of-the-century" home—which is real estate terminology for "very old house."

Phil often said he could never add materials to her of anywhere near the quality he had taken from her. I, on the other hand, was sure that General Sherman was so smitten he ordered her spared as he burned his was through Georgia. (For you history buffs, I realize Sherman went through before our house was built, but I like to think that if he *had* seen her, he would have spared her.)

"Honey," I heard Phil call. "I checked inside and out. There is no fire. The smoke alarm seems to have malfunctioned in the cold. It was a false alarm."

I herded the children back to bed, put on a pot of coffee and tried to calm down. A few minutes later Phil came in with a curious look on his face. "Honey, what is that on the front lawn?"

"It's our valuables. That's all I could think to salvage in a hurry."

"Gaye," he said slowly, "there is *nothing* of mine in there."

I hate to admit what I had gathered up in that bedspread and hastily appraised as valuable. My make-up was in there, but not my Bible. My curlers, but not pictures of the family. My jewelry, but no important papers. Need I go on? Just my stuff.

In retrospect, I'm not so sure that night was a "false alarm." I'm convinced it was designed as a wake-up call to my heart. If Jesus were to peek into that bundle today, would He say, "There is nothing of MINE in there?"

Might not hurt for us to take a look.

Chapter Four

I'll Tune to His Frequency—
Right After This Song

I was flying along on a clear day, content to enjoy the view and the quiet. Then I realized it wasn't really quiet; the controller's voice continuously crackled over the radio. Since I knew my assigned heading and there were no storm clouds in sight, I decided to check if there was anything else on the radio. I fiddled with the dial and suddenly the mellow sounds of jazz filled the cockpit. Pretty cool. I found out you can be at four or five thousand feet and tune in to a local radio station.

As a pilot you learn early about wavelengths and radio frequencies. With a switch of the dial you can replace the controller's voice with one that is more entertaining. Had there been another plane in my vicinity...or a sudden squall...

Tuning out the controller can be a risky decision.

Express Line to Nowhere

I was reminded of the importance of staying on the Lord's "wavelength" while standing in the express line at Shop & Grow Old. You can have a birthday standing in the express line at the grocery store. I am convinced you can form *intimate* friendships standing in the express line. I have known a few people that got engaged.

One day as I was standing there, the retired gentleman in front of me turned around and said, "Lady, would you like to know what happened to me last week?"

I said, "Oh, yeah..." since I had already read all the Enquirer headlines. After all, the real scoop is on the inside, which means you either have to buy one, or stand behind someone who is reading one. If you do get caught reading a tabloid, you're obligated to declare it "trash."

But trash can be oh, so tempting. To escape the temptation, I said, "Tell me what happened to you last week."

"Somebody stole eighty dollars worth of groceries from my glove compartment."

"I believe it. What was it, a pound of bacon?"

Isn't it amazing how quickly our attention can be diverted? There is a smorgasbord, if you will, of information whirling around us all the time. It courts our attention and attempts to drive our behavior. From billboards to musak, we are bombarded with the long bony finger of marketing. What is it that baits us, and influences our decision to tune in to that message?

Are You Listening to the Right Voices?

I never thought about billboards until a few years ago. I used to get in my car and listen to an encouraging tape, or talk to the Lord about things in my life that needed sorting out. It was a time to interact and listen. Today it angers me to see those pornographic billboards. It bothers me that they have license to blatantly reach over the highway and grab my attention. Then I am forced to re-negotiate my thoughts to bring them back where they belong.

The same thing is true with television. Phil and I have been married forever—he is older than dirt, after all—but there are commercials on television that make me blush.

They not only make me uncomfortable, they constitute an assault, in my opinion.

The radio bothers me sometimes. There are certain stores in the mall I can't shop in, because I can't stand the music for any length of time. I have approached many a clerk and said, "This is the neatest store, but I cannot shop here. Your window display calls me in, but your music drives me out." The response is usually, "We play it because it's popular."

"Not with my generation, Sugar, and we have the money."

Or have you been in a restaurant, and halfway through your salad you begin to notice the background music? By the time the entree is served, you want to take that speaker and throw it into the parking lot. Do you know it is designed to do that to you? It is their way of guaranteeing you don't sit there for three hours and leave a dollar tip. They don't want you lingering; they want you out of there as soon as your meal is eaten. Subtle control from a channel you never even tuned in.

I have often found myself in the grocery store humming a little ditty, only to realize it is part of a commercial—for beer, dog food, or worse.

I tell my students "feel free to unplug." From the time we get up until we go to bed at night, we are attached with an umbilical cord to the TV, radio, internet or cell phone. Even in our church services, we seem terrified of silence. When the heavens are silent, it is not evidence that the heavens are vacant. Quite possibly it is a sign that God can't get a word in edgewise.

It would probably shock us how much He has to say, if we could just listen. Next time you are in the car, unplug and listen. He will bombard you with insight and flashes of wisdom that will take your breath away. He will tell you where He stands on an issue. A few of the things He has told me:

- Pry your fingers off what you have committed to Me.
- You have eloquently defined the problem. Can you as eloquently declare the victory?
- If your work *for* Me has taken you away from time *with* Me, you are too busy.
- Are you going to do this, or am I?

How do I know that was God's voice? Believe me, I would not have told me that. I feel so strongly about being selective regarding the channels we tune into. What you listen to has the power to resurface at will and do an instant replay. If what you tune in is positive, you have a gold mine stored inside. If, on the other hand, you tune in to your baser instincts, you have a problem. No wonder Job said in chapter 31:1a "I have made a covenant with mine eyes."

I am reminded of a story I heard long ago. A man said to his friend, "I sometimes feel there is a white dog and a black dog warring inside me." His friend asked, "Who wins?"

"The one I feed the most."

I don't know the origin of that story, but it graphically illustrates my point. As surely as my long ago flight instructor's voice surfaces even today, I know my heavenly Father's voice will have far more residual value if I stay tuned in.

Being God's Voice to Others

There are times in our lives, though, when it is so hard to stay tuned in. For me, it was hardest to hear the Controller's voice during my children's teenage years. It's a wonder I can still hear anything at all. But I can testify that Jesus has seen me through. You come through fat, but you do come through. I am a little fluffy because when my children were teens, I turned to prayer and eclairs. There is nothing that prayer and eclairs don't help. If you are a skinny Mom of teenagers, you probably need to spend more time at the bakery.

The Lord saw me through those years when they're 12 and 13 and want the whole world to think they're adopted. That's okay; **you** want the whole world to think they're adopted. In fact, when mine were about 14, I would say to them, "We're going to find your real mother, and she's going to finish raising you." We'd go to the mall and I'd say, "See that lady in navy and pink? That's your mother. Go hug her."

They're all in therapy, but we're doing fine.

He's seen me through those years when my oldest son worked for the telephone company. He only lived seven miles from me, but I'd never see him; he was so busy. I can't tell you how many times I almost wrecked my car waving at phone trucks. One day I decided to go down to the phone company, right past the "No Trespassing" sign, and find his personal truck. I put this note on his windshield. "You were not hatched from an egg. Guess who?"

He called me that afternoon.

The Lord has seen me through those years when my youngest son called me collect to wish me Happy Mother's Day. I cried all morning long because he hadn't called, and all afternoon because he had.

He's the same child that when he married, he married in a tuxedo and tennis shoes. People said, "I understand you're the mother of the groom."

"No, she wasn't able to be with us today, but she's a nice lady."

I'm beginning to believe what Mark Twain said. "When a child is born, we must put them in a barrel, and drill a hole in it so they can breathe. When they are 13, you must put a cork in the hole."

God also got us through Steven's graduation. Now Steven is, tuxedo-tennis shoes, call-collect-to- wish-you-happy-mother's-day. When Steven graduated from High School, I don't have space to tell you what we were going through, other than to say I was quoting daily, "God looketh on the heart, not the hair." I've actually had people ask me where that scripture can be found. It's one you have to write in the margin. You would never have picked him up on the highway, because he looked like he'd mug you. But he was a neat kid. Only thing was, you couldn't talk to him about spiritual things. A lot like his mother at that age.

I'd say to him, "Steve, how long are we going to go through this?"

And he'd say, "Mom, it is a statement I am making, and I'm almost through."

To which I'd respond, "And I'm almost dead, okay?"

Now unfortunately, when Steven graduated from high school, he was not through making his statement. You know how you get together on a football field or in an auditorium and clap for yours when they come down to get their diploma? That's important so you don't mess with their psyche.

We were in the stands on the football field, and I have to tell you, Steven was beautiful. He looked a lot like his sister, but he was beautiful. When he came down to get his diploma, a lady behind me gasped, "Oh, that's a *guy!*"

Now what would you have done? I punched Phil and said, "Clap for the next five kids, and nobody will know the hippie is ours." So that's what we did.

God is not done with me, and God is not done with my family. When I stay tuned in to His voice, He gives me strength and hope. When one of my sons planted carrots in the garden, he would go out every day and pull them up to see how much they had grown. I have done that so many times. I check on those I love every day to see if my words have grown roots. The process doesn't work on my timetable, though. It is a comfort to know that when you are planting His word, you are assured of a harvest. Isaiah 55:11 says, "So shall my word be that goeth forth out of my mouth; it shall not return unto me void, but it shall accomplish that which I please, and it shall prosper in the things where to I sent it."

Wow, the marketing world would love to have that kind of guarantee when it sets forth to grab out attention.

Are you tuned in to God's frequency? Are you listening to His voice?

Chapter Five

Must the Controller Have His Finger
in *Every* Part of My Trip?

One day my instructor and I were practicing "touch and go's." I would circle the airport, land, and then take off and do it all over again. After about an hour, I lined up on the final leg of the next landing, my instructor encouraging me from the next seat. "Perfect, perfect. Now all you have to do is give it a little back pressure so we don't fly into the ground. Back pressure...baaaaack presssssure...BEND YOUR ELBOW, STUPID!" At his shout I started to cry and would have flown the plane into the ground if he had not been with me.

Though I was grateful for his presence in situations like that, in the back of my mind was still the thought, *this too shall pass, and then I will be on my own*. The day finally came when he crawled out of the plane after my last lesson and released his tether on me.

On my next trip, I got quite a shock. I realized the tether had not been removed. Rather, it had been handed over to the air traffic controller—and his involvement was permanent. I would never graduate from his control. As long as I wanted to occupy space in the sky, I would have to clear every flight and all its details with him.

In the beginning I resented his rather insistent finger in every aspect of my trip, but I have learned to welcome his presence. In the same way, our heavenly Controller reaches to the place where we are, whether in the air or on the ground.

The type of instruction given is determined by the situation. There are times the controller adds the phrase "at pilot's discretion." That is a term sometimes used when issuing clearance. It simply means you have some latitude as to *when*—not if—you comply with the issued instructions. Let me illustrate it this way.

"Does Your Mother Know You Are Out in Traffic?"

I was on my way to the health spa one day, and I was in a hurry. I had a class to teach at the college, and I wanted to go by the health spa beforehand. I looked behind me and saw a little blue light flashing. Ugh, I hate when that happens. So I slowed down, pulled over, and reached around and clicked in my seat belt. I know you don't ever do that.

A policeman came around to my car and said, "May I see your driver's license?"

"Yes, sir."

I said "Sir" because I found out they don't like you to call them "Sugar." Although I don't know why they mind, because they all look like they're nine-years-old, to me. I just want to say, "Does your Mom know you're playing cop?" Because you know, there they are with a gun, and they're in traffic and everything.

"Mrs. Martin," he asked, "Are you aware of how fast you were going?"

"No sir, I'm not."

"Well, you were exceeding the speed limit, and I'm going to have to write you a ticket." As he handed me the ticket he said, "Mrs. Martin, I see you're aware of our seat belt law."

"Yes, sir, I am."

He said, "Let me ask you, Mrs. Martin, do you *always* buckle your seat belt through the steering wheel?"

"Not always."

We may chuckle at that little story, but there are times the controller gives you no choice in complying with his instructions, or in the timing of your compliance. You are issued an order to "descend and maintain flight level 2400 immediately." All choices are vetoed; you are expected to comply *immediately*. Sometimes our heavenly Controller tells us to "Trust me. Now." No warning, and no explanations are given. Such was the case in our family some years back.

The Gift of Christy and Laurie

Through this set of circumstances, God taught our family that the richness of the walk is in complying when you have no choice in the matter. I work with companies every day that count all their benefits in dollars. The buzz word for years has been the *bottom line,* and that line is punctuated with a dollar sign. After our experience, I'm convinced that true identity is forged in what we *give away*. Proverbs 11:24 (TLB) says, "It is possible to grow rich by giving away."

My brother and his wife had a little girl named Christy. Their third daughter, Christy came down with a devastating heart problem at the age of seven. My brother and his wife are fine Christian people, and they went to the Lord and claimed Christy's healing and full recovery. But when Christy was eight years old, she died. She weighed less than twenty pounds.

Her death devastated our family. During this time I learned first-hand the power of the scripture in 2 Corinthians 1:6-7 TLB. "...In our trouble God has comforted us—and this too to help you: to show you from our personal experience how God will tenderly comfort you when you undergo these same sufferings. He will give you the strength to endure."

Phil and I went down and spent ten days with my brother and his family. Every time I tried to offer comfort, my brother would say, "You don't know what we are going through." He was right; I didn't know. Though I loved Christy, my relationship with her was different from the one my brother and his wife had with her. I could not comfort him. But if you had come to my brother and said, "Mr. Foster, we lost a child," he would have responded, because he knew you had been where he was.

Doctors told us that there was no evidence in medical documentation that this disease had ever been in a family more than once. We honestly felt at the time that the disease was viral. All the geneticists and immunologists involved told us the same thing.

A few years later, Betty became pregnant with another child. We were just thrilled. It was the first time there was a new breath of hope for their lives, and it brought them out of a terrible grief. Laurie was born—a wonderful little gift to our family.

When she was seven, her parents took her to the doctor for a minor illness, only to discover she had the same disease Christy had. The cry of our hearts was "Why? WHY?

After several weeks of hearing us question God, my eighty-six-year-old mother finally had enough. "Why NOT us?" she demanded. "What is there so special about our family that God can't cross our path with adversity? What is there so special about us that God can't give and God can't take? And if He did not bring this to us, who would you have Him take it to?"

The hard questions she asked convinced me anew that this was not a situation of "pilot's discretion." Obedience to God's plan and trust in His wisdom was not optional. Our job was not to understand; it was to trust Him. He had brought these circumstances into our lives; it was our job to keep flying and trust Him to bring us through the storm safely.

Ironically, Laurie came down with the disease in the same year—and month—of her life that Christy had. We now believe it may be a genetic disease. As word of her illness spread, doctors and immunologists came out of the woodwork, and geneticists from all over the world came out of retirement and called asking for samples of her blood.

In October, the doctors told us we needed to have as nice a Christmas as possible, because Laurie might not be with us for long. I will never forget that Christmas. The whole family got together and had a wonderful time. We partied hearty.

In January, the doctors told us there was an option open to us that had not been open when Christy was alive: a pediatric heart transplant. Pediatric transplants were not yet available when Christy passed away. The doctors told my brother and sister-in-law to think about it—but they only had two weeks to make a decision. Our whole family immediately went to prayer. That's a big decision to make for a little girl.

Laurie was eight years old then, and, at just twenty-seven pounds, she looked like a refugee. Her parents decided to go ahead with a heart transplant, and then interviewed several different hospitals around the country. They settled on Shands Hospital in Gainesville, Florida, mainly because Shands was close enough to us and to where they live, that they'd have family support. They felt that was important.

They put Laurie in Shands in late January. She was so sick she would vacillate on and off the candidacy list for a heart, because we couldn't keep her well enough to stay eligible every day. We did everything we could to keep her a candidate.

I don't know if you know anything about transplant programs, but they are an emotional roller coaster. We needed a heart, but we were not looking to purchase a heart, because you can't buy one. It doesn't make any difference how much money you have, you can't buy a heart. Someone has to *give* it to you.

Did you know that hearts have no gender? We were not looking for a female heart. We were looking for a heart.

And did you know there's no race to heart? We were not looking for a Caucasian heart. We were looking for a heart.

There were some prerequisites and criteria that had to be met and one of them was size. We had to have a heart from a twenty-five to forty-five pound donor. You know that means a very young child. How do you pray for a heart for someone you love, when you know your prayer can only be answered through someone else's tragedy?

It was an emotionally wrenching time.

On March 9 we had all been up to see Laurie in intensive care. It was 11:00 p.m. by the time we got home. Five minutes later the phone rang. It was the hospital. "You've got to come right back. We think we have a heart."

We were in the intensive care unit when Laurie's doctor, the head of the transplant program at Shands, woke her up and asked, "Laurie, do you want a heart?"

"Yes, sir."

"Do you want one tonight?"

"Yes, sir."

"Then I and my team are ready to get on a plane and go get you one."

That was an exciting time. The team stays in touch with you every fifteen minutes. "We're out at the Gainesville airport." "We're in the air." "We're fifteen minutes from the donor city."

They tell the recipient family very little. They tell the donor family a great deal more, because they have a greater need to know. We were never told the city they went to, but Phil's a retired air traffic controller, and he called out to the control tower and asked, "Where did the LifeFlight go?" They told him it was en route to New Orleans. Phil said, "It's going after a heart for my niece." They said, "Don't worry about it, we'll clear it all the way through when they head back." Controllers don't normally do that, but they did it that night.

Later we heard, "We're fifteen minutes from the donor city." "We're on the ground." "We're in the ambulance." "We're in the hospital." And finally, "We have harvested the heart."

When we heard that message, they took Laurie into the operating room, opened her up and put her on by-pass. However, they do not sever the old heart until the new heart is in the operating room, barring accident.

I don't know if I can express the enormous intensity of that moment. The intensity of the joy, knowing when the pilot steps out of that helicopter with an igloo cooler, he's carrying brand new life for someone you love. Or the intensity of the grief, knowing that some family in New Orleans saw that same igloo cooler leave with the last vestige of life of someone they loved.

Laurie got her heart.

Phil and I were among the first to see her after she came out of surgery for her transplant. I have the same blood type, so I gave blood for her. "Laurie, look, Aunt Gaye gave blood. I didn't cry or anything. You're going to have hips tomorrow!"

She doesn't. She weighs 84 pounds now and is a wonderful young lady.

We're all born with a bad heart. Sometimes it doesn't kick up and betray us until we're a little ways into life. But it will. You can't buy a new one. Somebody had to die to give you one. And that somebody was Jesus.

One thing we've learned with Laurie is that she will spend the rest of her life fighting rejection. I don't know about you, but I got my new heart as a young mother many years ago. I have spent a great deal of time in the days since fighting rejection. My old sinful nature desperately wants to reject this new heart, and fights me daily for control.

It is possible to grow rich by giving away. My family is rich indeed. There is a family in New Orleans richer than we. This man Jesus brought riches into our lives that we could never have gotten for ourselves.

We were not, and are not, the only ones that have been issued instructions we did not understand, or want to comply with. Like the controller in his tower, God does not expect us to understand, or even agree with the instructions He gives us. He does expect our obedience. Generations ago there was a similar situation with a man called Jehoshaphat.

Why Not You?

In 2 Chronicles 20, we get quite a lesson in how to handle the surprise attack. Jehoshaphat woke up one morning and discovered he was surrounded by the enemy. I have a feeling that as he looked out over his foes, he might have asked, "Why me? Why now?"

Sometimes it is a major leap of faith from the news that you are surrounded, to the reminder that "No weapon that is formed against thee shall prosper" (Isaiah 54:17a).

When I was praying about this, the Lord said to me, "Gaye, when you pray, I bend down and lend my ear to your cause. When you pray, angels pack for a trip, and war is waged. When you pray, the heavenly host hold their breath for my command. When you pray, strongholds begin to crumble, and I send assistance. When you pray, new construction begins and I'll bring beauty out of ashes."

He gives us His assurance in Isaiah 43:2: "When thou passest through waters, I will be with thee and through the rivers they shall not overflow thee: when thou walkest through the fire, thou shalt not be burned; neither shall the flame kindle upon thee."

God's Formula for Handling Crisis

Jehoshaphat was getting ready to learn three things. First, he would learn his limitations. He didn't know what to do, so he called a prayer meeting. Do you call a prayer meeting as soon as you come under attack? That is exactly the right response. We see that example all through the Scriptures. It says Jehoshaphat feared and set himself to seek the Lord.

Do you also know that it's perfectly normal to fear? Jesus said, "Fear not" more often than he said anything else. Sometimes the facts will overwhelm you. But it's okay to fear, if it drives you to your knees to seek the Lord. When I'm afraid, I hit my knees in the hallway, slide all the way into the bedroom and say, "God, its Gaye."

Fear frees you to "crisis pray." Jehoshaphat hit his knees and told God, "We have no might against this great company that cometh against us. Neither know we what to do..."

The Word "But"

"...But our eyes are on you." After Jehoshaphat confessed his weakness, he focused on the source of his strength.

Let me give you a wonderful truth that comes out of my communications class. It's this little word: "but." Anytime you see this word, anytime you hear it anyplace, it negates everything that was said before it, and screams that the real message is still to come.

If I were to say to you, "Phil is a wonderful husband, and we have had so many good years together, but I'm thinking seriously about running off to Jamaica with the gardener." What would you remember? Jamaica-gardener.

This word negates everything that was said before. It doesn't matter if you hear it on television, read it in the Bible, or anywhere else, it screams that the real message comes after it.

Let's look at it this way. I can't tell you how many times people say to me, "You have such a pretty face but—" Don't hurt me. Because I know what they're going to say, "—but you could lose some weight." Or "I loved your seminar, but—"

You see. If that is true, then think of the time Jesus said to Peter, "Satan has desired to have you, to sift you as wheat." I'll tell you, if Jesus had said that to me, it would be hard for me to let go of that. Jesus didn't stop there, though. He said, "But, I have prayed for you." That's the real message. "I have prayed for you that your faith fail you not." That's where the real message is.

Jehoshaphat said, "We have no might against this great company. Neither know we what to do, *but* our eyes are on you."

Learning from Jehoshaphat

Our eyes are on you. Jehoshaphat learned his limitations, and he focused on the source of his strength. Very often in order to get our eyes back on him, God allows the situations in our life to spin out of our control. He is a master at doing that. At the very instant Jehoshaphat put this problem in God's hands and said, "Our eyes are on you," at that very instant, the Word of God leapt from the throne of heaven into Jehoshaphat's ear in a prophecy.

Listen to what he said in verse 15: "Be not afraid, nor dismayed by reason of this great multitude, for the battle is not yours, but God's. You shall not need to fight in this battle. Set yourselves. Stand still, see the salvation of the Lord. Fear not, nor be dismayed. Tomorrow, go ye out against them, for the Lord will be with you. Believe in the Lord, so shall you be established. Believe in his prophets, so shall ye prosper."

Wow, what a mouthful. Where is the key word in all of that? It looks like there is more than one. Stand still. Fear not. Go out and believe in the Lord. There is no doubt you need to read the chapter. In my Bible, this passage is underlined and dated numerous times when those exact words were what I needed to win the victory. But let's be honest: it is far more exciting to hear that passage, than to try to be obedient to it. It is easier to rejoice with someone else's victory, than to trust God with the outcome of our own struggles and enemy attacks.

Obey God to the Letter

Jehoshaphat's last lesson was to obey *to the letter* what God told him to do. That sounds easy until God tells you to do it. God told him there was an enormous army out here, and instead of sending out his troops, he should send the choir. We have a great choir in our church, but I wouldn't send our choir to do battle. I am sure Jehoshaphat thought, "How can it be? How can it be?"

God said, "Send the choir."

I see a lot of truth in here. I honestly believe that if we would send forth more praise in the face of the attack, we would have the victory a lot sooner. Psalm 22:3 reminds us that God inhabits our praise. Isaiah 61:3 says that we have been given the garment of praise for the spirit of heaviness. I can feel a song welling up now, can't you? I can feel the heaviness lifting, and can see God moving into the midst of the battle.

Have you ever asked, "Why me? Why now?" We know why. Because we're not our own. I Corinthians 6:20a tells us we are bought with a price. The Father always has our best interests at heart. With that in mind, the voice of the Controller is not nearly as intimidating or threatening as it would be if we had no glimpse of His plan.

I have also learned, that at least for this pilot, "pilot's discretion" is often flawed. Therefore, my prayer is "You issue it, Lord, and I'll do my best to comply with it."

"Jesus, thank you so much for your faithfulness. We want you to know, Lord, we love you. We want you to do with us everything you've determined to do. We ask you to deafen your ears to our murmurings. We ask you to come, and if you have to come on the wings of the attack, then come. We ask you Jesus, to use whatever means it takes to finish the work in us that you've begun."

Chapter Six

When You're Cleared for Take-Off, It's Not Cool if You Don't Go Anywhere

Some years back, a friend flew with me out of Wilmington, Delaware. I made very sure I listened closely to the controller so I wouldn't miss it when he cleared us for take-off. As you know by now, I learned firsthand that it is not cool if he issues clearance—and you stay parked on the runway.

No sooner had we gotten in the air, that we got into such fog I could not see a thing. Nothing. That is a DANGEROUS place to be if you are not fully qualified to fly in marginal weather. I was not. I was marginally qualified for clear days. They call that kind of poor visibility "socked in," and I think it has something to do with what you stuff in your mouth to stifle the screams.

As usual, I decided to use the "fake-it-till-you-make-it" approach. I dropped lower and lower, trying to see the ground. Keep in mind that I had no idea where the trees or towers were in this area. They are marked on the map, but you have to have a general idea of where you are in order to read the map. Finally, finally, between the clouds and fog, I saw a small dirt runway. There were tall pine trees on one end of it, and a field with cattle on the other. I decided to land from the end where the field was, and then wait on the ground until the weather cleared.

I was so determined to get *on* the ground before I fell *to* the ground, that I came in low, low, low. Have you ever seen cows on their knees? Have you ever seen them hold hands and pray? I have. When we rolled up to the little building at the end of the runway, we saw an old gentleman sitting on the porch in a rocker. "Well, ladies," he said, taking a piece of straw from between his teeth, "I doubt they will ever give milk again." He looked us up and down and then asked, "Do you know where you are?"

I wanted to say, "Of course I do." I knew I was on the ground; what more was there to know. Though I wanted to keep up appearances, I finally did admit I was lost. Bluffing while standing on the ground is dangerous—but can be fatal in the air.

Appearance Management 101

Cosmetics, a fake-it-till-you-make-it attitude, and making good first impressions are all part of what we call "appearance management." Jesus talked a lot about appearance management, only He called it what it really is: hypocrisy. In Matthew 23:27(NIV) He said, "...You look like whitewashed tombs, which look beautiful on the outside but on the inside are full of dead men's bones and everything unclean."

We live in a society where a greater value is put on the cosmetics of things than on their true condition. I fight against that in my own life. It is far more important today that you look fit, than be fit. For instance, let's talk about girdles. If the ad says that to wear one will "take off ten pounds," I buy four and wear them all at the same time. According to my calculations that should be good for forty pounds.

My mother said to me one day, "You're putting on a little weight."

I was, because at that time, we had our grown children back at home living with us. There was nothing in Dr. Spock to prepare us for that. There was barely enough in Isaiah to get us through it. Before they moved out, my daughter said to me, "Mother, would you potty train Stephie?"

"Sure," I said. It's no big deal. We potty trained our children with Ande's candies. Every time you tinkled you got an Ande's candy. It only took two days.

So when mother commented on my weight, I said, "I know. I've just potty trained Stephie. Now every time I go, I eat a Mounds bar."

Finally my mother said, "You need a girdle."

"Mother, please."

She said, "You are not walking behind you."

"That is not my problem." I fix up the front really great, and don't worry about what's in the back.

This conversation drove me to the mall, where this little teensy girl waited on me. Why is it always a teensy little girl? It's just revolting. I waited until I thought no one else was around and whispered, "I need to see a girdle."

"Sure," she chirped. "In what size?"

I leaned in close and said, "XXXXL."

"Four X's?" she shrieked. It was like E.F. Hutton had spoken. Everybody turned to look.

"Please," I begged.

"Have you ever tried a large?"

"Uh, huh. Gives me gangrene in my legs."

I have climbed out of my plane or into my girdle many a time with one thing in mind—to make a good impression. Please don't misunderstand. There is nothing wrong with wanting to look together and competent. The problem is when that becomes our main focus. When we spend so much time worrying about the outside that we neglect things like character and integrity; then it is a problem.

And often, how you handle a less than perfect impression says more about you than how you look in all four undergarments, or if you blew the perfect landing.

First Impressions

One day the consulting firm I worked for called and said they needed me to fly to Atlanta to conduct a seminar with all gentlemen. I dropped to my knees and thanked God for answering my prayers. I mean, what else could be so wonderful? I flew into Atlanta, checked into my hotel, and checked out the next morning in my navy blue suit, white blouse, and navy and white spectators. Does that sound together? It certainly ought to. *Dress for Success* says that it is. I knew I would make the right impression. My clients were gentlemen from the banking community— among them sixteen million-dollar sellers in real estate. We met in the executive suite of one of the savings and loan buildings. I was unaware they had executive suites, but take my word for it, the executive suites are nicer than the lobbies. I use a blackboard a great deal in my work, and every time I turned around that morning to write on the board, these men snickered.

Now I had checked myself to be sure I was not in my jammies, and I wasn't. Finally I said to them, "Gentlemen, we have to spend four hours together this morning. I need to know what's funny." By the way, my topic that day was: Making yourself marketable.

They said, "You have a pink curler in the back of your hair." I don't know how I did that. My credibility went right down the tubes.

I later received one of the nicest plaques from them. Insurance people and bankers will send you the nicest plaques. It was made of mahogany, with a little brass plate on it. They had inscribed it "For the most unique presentation," and had glued a pink sponge curler to it. It hangs in our laundry room. Way, way back in the laundry room.

God Looks at the Heart

Not long after that I began to pray, "Lord, teach me how to behave as your child in every set of circumstances." Then I sat back and waited on Him to send me a book. He didn't send a book, He sent some situations to teach me how to behave as His child.

My grandson, Christopher, was only about a year and a half old then, and he had spent a couple of weeks with us. My plan was to fly to Atlanta to give him back to his mother, and then fly on to Jacksonville to speak to a group there. As I walked through the airport in Gainesville, I realized everyone else seemed to be carrying tennis rackets and suntan lotion, while I was hauling a diaper bag, and had fruit loops in my hair.

Since my daughter worked for Eastern at the time, I was pass riding and thought, *I don't know if I'm going to make it on this plane or not.*

Christopher and I did make it on the plane, I turned him over to his mother, and then checked in for my flight to Jacksonville. The girl behind the ticket counter said, "I don't think I'm going to be able to get you on this flight."

"Listen," I said, "I have to speak to a group in Jacksonville. I'll ride in the bathroom if I have to, but I have to get on this plane."

"We'll do what we can."

So I got out my *Reader's Digest* and sat over in the corner while they boarded the rest of the plane, because pass riders are the last to board. I should have gone into the restroom and fixed up, but I didn't. There I was, fruit loops in my hair, and looking like a truck had run over me. I mean, please, two weeks with a grandchild. I didn't have enough time to shave both legs on the same day.

A few minutes later I heard the agent call my name.

I looked up and she said, "I have one seat left."

"You're kidding me."

"It's in first class."

Wow.

"And," she said, "I have the nicest treat for you. You know who you're riding next to?"

"Who?"

"Pat Boone."

Pat Boone? I was going to sit next to Pat Boone with fruit loops in my hair? Do you know how hard it is to behave as His child in that set of circumstances?

Pat Boone asked me, "What do you do?"

I mumbled, "Uh, nothing."

There was just no way I could tell Pat Boone I was a consultant.

That day I prayed the cabin lights would go out to spare Pat Boone the shock—and me the embarrassment. But I can tell you that when you are in the cockpit, if there is anything you want to function, it is the lights. The lights on the control panel and gauges illuminate all the important information necessary to make that flight a safe one. When there is an electrical problem and you aren't sure how much fuel you have or the status of the systems on the plane, you get a little—no, a lot—nervous. Light has amazing properties to reveal the true condition of a matter.

Turn Out the Light

About a week or two before I left for another speaking engagement, I decided to go to Gainesville to get a couple of cute outfits. You know, important stuff. I had already prayed about what I would say and felt I knew what the Lord wanted me to do. So I went to Gainesville and was shopping around and went into Maas Brothers. They had this cute little thing working at the Estee Lauder counter who said, "Would you like a make-over?"

"Oh, why not. Sure."

She took all my make-up off, and then she turned on a bright light—with a magnified mirror— and I saw myself in a way I had never seen myself before. It was shocking. I don't think I'm that vain, but I guess maybe I am, because as soon as I saw my face under that kind of light I said, "You know what, Sugar, I have an appointment I totally forgot about." And I got out of there.

On the way home I was listening to my tapes, when the spirit of the Lord spoke to me and said, "I was in that."

"You were in what?"

"Gaye, I was in that situation with the mirror."

He said, "Because when that spotlight illuminated your flaws and left you vulnerable, you backed away real quick. You adjust the intensity of the light—and your proximity to it—to the exact degree it makes you look good."

Ouch. Let me say it again. "You adjust the intensity of the light—and your proximity to it, to the exact degree it makes you look good."

After I used that illustration at a Bible study a lady said to me, "How do you know God told you that?"

I said, "Ma'am, I would not have said that to me. It was God."

Haven't we all done that? We try to get away from the spotlight, for fear of not making a good impression. We say no when we're asked to teach, because we're afraid we won't be any good at it. We don't greet new people at church for fear they'll say "We've been members since 1979." We hide our true selves for fear of rejection. Or worse yet, we don't pray or read the Bible because we're afraid God will hold His light up to our hearts and see all the things we try to hide.

But you know what, God sees it all anyway. The amazing thing is that God loves us—and Jesus died for us—just the way we are. Though He hates our sin, He loves us, unconditionally. With that knowledge we can step out and risk looking foolish. Don't let appearance management keep you from hearing His voice and being who He wants you to be.

Part II
Chapters Seven - Ten

**Lifetime Enrollment in God's Flight School
(or, Learning to Listen—Even
When We Don't Want To)**

Gaye Martin

Chapter Seven

A Good Instructor Takes the Terror Out of Flying "Solo"

Since I'm firstborn, it is real important for me to tell my parents about any achievements I make. That's true of firstborn children. So the day I got my pilot's license, I immediately went down to Pan Am Airlines where my father worked. "Dad, I have my pilot's license!" I cried. I was SO excited, because my father was a pilot, and at that time, he was also the training director for Pan Am.

He looked at me and said, very solemnly, "Honey, you are more dangerous today than you've ever been in your life."

I was crushed, just crushed. "Why?" I asked.

"Because today you think you have all the answers."

Several years later, Phil and I began flying supplies to missionaries. Our first flight would take us over Cuba enroute to Columbia—in a single engine plane. My father was devastated when he heard what we had planned. We wouldn't do it again today, but that was all God gave us. And a single engine beat no engine at all.

When I told Dad about the trip, he said, "It is just so, so stupid to do that."

I wasn't sure how to respond. I had expected him to say something like, "God will get you there and back safely." So I stammered, "Well...we have life jackets on board..."

"You know what that means?" he shouted. "It means the bodies will float!"

Those were hard words, but oh, so valuable. We made extra sure the engine was in top shape, prayed hard, and thought a bit more before we accepted other assignments. You see, a good instructor doesn't just tell you what you want to hear, he tells you what you need to hear. Our instructors, whether formal or informal, have such an affect on our lives.

More than once the Lord has put me in a situation that required an instructor. It costs a little more to get private instruction, but in the long run it is far less expensive than correcting your solo mistakes.

Rafting to Glory

For example, one summer I took my daughter, Fran, and granddaughter, Stephanie, and rented a cabin in North Carolina for a week. Our family often takes separate vacations. Phil and the guys go somewhere like Canada and do guy things, and I take some of the girls, and we go do girl things—like shopping.

One day, though, Stephanie said, "Nanie, I want to whitewater raft."

"I don't think so."

"Oh, come on, Nanie."

My argument was, "I am painting this memory picture, and I don't see a raft anywhere in it." It is my belief that if we are using my credit card, then I am painting the picture. However, the two of them talked me into a day of whitewater rafting. It wasn't pretty. It amazes me that you have to sign a release for something called "recreation."

I found out there are two ways you can go down the river. One is with a guide, and the trip is about three hours. The other way is without a guide, and the trip takes three months. I insisted on a guided trip.

Ladies, let me tell you, if I had known you could rent a man for thirty-eight dollars a day, I would never have married twice.

Anyway, we rented Ken. Ken was just about my age, but he was in much better shape. As I stood there in my bathing suit with my life jacket on, I decided I needed to bond with Ken.

"Now Ken," I said, "I realize I don't look like a professional right now. I look like Shamu in latex. But I am a professional. And I'm going to write a letter when this trip is over. Because I teach communications skills at the college level, I have the power to write a letter that will make you big money if you publish it. I could also write a letter to the editor of the newspaper that will close your business, if they print it. So if I were you, I'd be really nice to the fat lady."

Our rafting trip took about four hours and we had a wonderful time. Ken proved to be a terrific guide. By the time we got out of the raft, he and I were almost engaged.

The Magic of a Good Teacher

Each of my instructors, from my father to Ken, had his own style. Some used repetition, others intimidation, and then there were those with the gift of motivating you far beyond your wildest expectations. Rather than critique every mistake, they applauded every effort. They coaxed and encouraged, and they had MAGIC.

Magic fascinates me. My response from rabbits to ropes is wow! Double wow! *How do they do that?* When you can make an elephant, the Statue of Liberty and a Boeing 747 disappear, the obvious question is, "How does that work?"

Somebody teach me, please, since I have two people—and my hips—that I want to make disappear.

They tell me magic is just an illusion. I don't care what they call it; they manage to fool me. Magic for me would be getting both legs in my pantyhose in under an hour.

But finding a magical formula to motivate us all is as deceptive as the claim, "One size fits all." There is no such thing; it's an illusion. I'm sure you've seen "magical" books at the bookstore: *Parenting in Three Easy Steps*. Excuse me? Or, *Lose Forty Pounds in Forty Minutes*. Then there is *Marriage: Locked in Love* and *Divorce: Opportunity for Personal Growth* by the same author. How about *Menopause—I can Grow a Beard in an Afternoon*, or *From Heathen to Heaven in one Weekend*.

You get the picture. It's getting any of this material to work that's the trick. I have tried incentives of all kinds and have even won some prizes designed to motivate my own performance level. I once won a cruise. That was right up there with dental surgery. The weather was so rough each meal was a roller coaster ride, and the walls were so thin you could hear hair grow. Some prize! I'm not motivated by cruises any more.

I also won a Pop-Up camper. Phil loved it so much; he camped in the back yard. I have yet to see the adventure in rolling over in bed and finding your nose hanging over the pilot light, or frying bacon sitting on your bed in your nightgown.

As I look back at those who motivated me, I think of two of my aunts. I doubt either "teacher" consciously intended to impact my life in a profound way, yet they left their fingerprints all over me. Only one of those teachers had magic.

The summer I was eight, I had a tonsillectomy. While recuperating, I decided to write love notes to several folks, including both my aunts. I delivered the first one to Aunt

Rose. "How nice dear, thank you so much," she replied. Before I left that day, I saw my note in the little trash can beside her dresser. From her I learned that rejection is a powerful teacher. I never felt the same about her. Because she questioned the value of my creativity, I immediately began to question my worth and value, to her at least.

Several days later we were invited to Aunt Irene's for dinner. I desperately fought the urge to give her the note. After all, it was written on Pan Am Airlines note paper and she was ever so much more sophisticated than Aunt Rose. She didn't have children of her own, so instead of jelly glasses she had crystal. She loved antiques and an invitation to her house called every formal bone and fiber to attention. She invested her finest into every visit, signaling oh, so eloquently that you were special, and this was an important visit.

I stood in her parlor, all starched and straight. As I slipped my note into Aunt Irene's hand, she stopped to read it. "I lighk you, you are so good. Love, Gaye."

"What a wonderful and thoughtful gift you have given me. I shall treasure it always." She framed it, and it sat on her antique table for years. In fact, I fell heir to it after she died at eighty-nine years of age.

From her I learned that acceptance and approval are not only powerful teachers, but great healers. From both aunts I learned that you create a climate for growth of one kind or another. The climate in Aunt Rose's home was tolerance, not acceptance. In Aunt Irene's home I was cultivated, polished and refined. She challenged my thoughts and my time and offered possible explanations for the shortcomings of others.

She also taught me to laugh. While she was watching her weight again, I once saw her devour three donuts. My Uncle commented, "I thought you were dieting."

"I am."

"Do you know how many donuts you ate?" he asked.

"Do you know how many I wanted?" she returned.

She was about eighty-four when she moved to a retirement village. When I went to visit and take her to lunch, she requested we walk to the car using the *outside* walkways. "The only thing I dislike about this place is the old people in the hallways," she confided.

She spun the magic of trust by giving her valuables into my care. The first endowment came when I was fifteen and had announced I was getting married. My mother immediately called in all the favors due her from family, friends, and anyone who walked slow, to try to convince me that a six-month delay would not turn me into a senior citizen with blue hair.

Aunt Irene invited me to supper, and I fully expected an argument about my upcoming marriage. Instead, she served a lovely meal and then said, "Before you go, I have a gift for you." A gift? She brought out a set of fine china dessert plates and put them in my hands. "You are entering a wonderful new phase of your life and I want to make a contribution to that new place. Use these when you entertain and enjoy them. You are a wonderful young lady and every young lady should begin her married life with a touch of fine china."

There she was, looking at things that were not, as though they were. She had reached past the rebellious exterior and grasped the latent woman in me, and she would never relinquish her. I could never be anything but ladylike around her. Her expectations demanded no less.

During each visit, she gave me something precious to her, along with the story of "how this piece came into my care." That attitude freed me from the greed that often accompanies possessions. She would say, "My dear, I have been thinking, and I do believe it is time for this piece to come live at your house. I am entrusting it to you for a season, and I'm sure you will know when it is time for it to grace another home. Enjoy it, use it, and get the thrill of passing it on."

Her tradition has come full circle now. I have had the thrill of saying to someone, "My dear, I have been thinking…"

Possibly the most dramatic sweep of her magic cape was the air of integrity that clung to everything she did. Someone once said, "The great big doors of success swing on little bitty hinges called integrity." Amen to that. I always considered myself a person with integrity, but being around Aunt Irene forced me to re-define integrity.

When independent living became difficult for Irene and her sister, they moved to a retirement village. Not long after, Irene's sister had a debilitating stroke and her assets were quickly depleted. Irene did not want to dip into her own reserves for fear she would later be a burden to the family. She was advised to apply for federal aid on her sister's behalf. The mere idea sent her into starched, stiff refusal. Finally, she gave in, and the agency subsidized her sister's care for two years.

A few months after her sister died, I found out Irene had begun making payments back to the agency. "You don't have to do that, Aunt Irene. You paid into the system and it is appropriate to take from it in this case." She was appalled. "My dear, if those of us who can pay it back, don't pay it back, the system will never work." I have no idea of the final outcome, but the lesson for me was learned.

When I think back on the impact Aunt Irene had on my life, I see the Lord's fingerprints all over that relationship. It was only a microscopic example of a much bigger picture.

I also learned much from Aunt Rose. Do you know someone that can brighten a room the minute they walk into it? And do you know people who can achieve the same goal by walking out of the room? You know what I mean. At one time or another, aren't we all surrounded with voices that belittle and demean? Voices that criticize and question our value and worth? Surely they come from the devourer of our souls. They so tamper with our sense of purpose that we become convinced we are not even desirable to our Lord. We are even tempted to think if we could just "clean up our act" THEN He would be pleased. Nonsense.

Thank God that "while we were yet sinners He loved us" (Romans 5:8b). He was the first to "look upon things that are not, as though they were"(Paraphrase of Romans 4:17). He sees beyond who we are to what we can be. He calls to our potential and woos it out of us, convincing us of all we can do and be when empowered by his Spirit. He whispers in our ear the great plans he has for us and where we fit into His plan.

His sheep hear his voice—they will not follow another. He can speak louder than the naysayers and shine bright enough to dispel the darkness that casts a long shadow over our path. When the world discards and trashes our pitiful attempts at reaching out for a relationship, He will frame our prayers and love notes and hide them close to his heart.

God used Aunt Irene in my life in powerful ways:

In her lessons of humor, He taught me joy;
In her lessons of trust, He taught me to lean;
In her model of selflessness, He taught me to give;
In her life of integrity, He taught me truth.
Maybe it's not magic at all; maybe it's LOVE.

Without a doubt all of my instructors changed my life in one way or another. I am indebted to the stern ones as much as I am to the more patient ones. In fact, the ones hardest to get along with motivated my determination to pass that lesson or training session. "Are you going to fly this plane like a man or a girl?" one instructor asked.

Another was so tough, after every lesson I checked to see if I had grown hair on my chest. He once told me to fix my face while he landed the plane. I fixed my face AND landed the airplane.

Don't ignore the instructors in your life. They may not always tell you what you *want* to hear, but be careful you don't ignore what you *need* to hear.

Chapter Eight

From Controlled Crashes to Smooth Landings—Easier Said Than Done

I don't know of a single pilot who made a perfect landing the first time out. Not surprisingly, my instructor referred to my first few landings as "controlled crashes." Smooth landings, like most everything else, take practice. Even when you have had lots of practice, they can still be rough sometimes.

Phil used to work as an air traffic controller in Gainesville, Florida, and he would chat with the flight crew if he had the chance. Once, while I was a passenger on a commercial flight from Atlanta to Gainesville, Phil told the pilot I was on board. Phil also mentioned that, as a frustrated small-aircraft pilot, I scrutinized and critiqued every landing.

When we approached the runway in Gainesville, the plane touched down, bounced, touched down again, and bounced several more times. After we finally settled on the runway, the pilot came over the intercom. "Mrs. Martin, how did you like those landings? The second was better than the first, don't you think?"

I knew then Phil had talked to him—and that this was a man who could roll with a few bad landings. I took more than a laugh away from that experience. I learned that most folks can tolerate a rough landing if you are transparent about your part in it. When we blow it, our Heavenly Controller picks us up and dusts us off, and points us back to the right heading. I have had to learn volumes to get to even a remotely smooth landing in various parts of my life. The place where I have had to practice the most is in marriage and parenting.

Conference Confrontations

People ask Phil and me all the time if we ever have any ripples in our marriage. I guess because we call each other "Sugar" all the time, people assume we never have problems. They don't realize we say "Sugar" because we can't always remember each other's name. "We don't have many ripples," I usually say, "but we HAVE had tidal waves." In fact, we have both been seasick on this sea of matrimony, and wondered why we ever signed up for the trip. A few times we wanted to get off the boat, but were too far out to swim back.

We have spoken at quite a few marriage retreats. Sometimes I thought that was like asking Mae West to speak on morality. I can't tell you the number of times just before were to show up with a word of wisdom for the people, we would have a knock-down, drag-out argument in our room. I mean, we weren't speaking to each other. I not only didn't want to be married to him anymore; I didn't want to be in the same room with him—much less pray with him. We'd walk into the meeting room and I'd whisper, "Smile, and look like you're happy."

"I am looking happy."

"You're not looking happy enough."

There were times when one of us wanted to say, "As soon as this marriage seminar is over, we're filing for divorce."

There were other times I said to God, "Send them a book, please, from someone perfect like Kay Arthur. I want to be like Kay Arthur. Kay Arthur's hair never has a hole in the back. Kay Arthur doesn't have an earring drop off when she is teaching. She never has a run in her hose, and she can stand under those lights and not sweat. I'm pretty sure she has never had an argument with her husband. I want to be off this ship and be like Kay Arthur."

Of course, God doesn't want me to spend time trying to be like Kay Arthur. He wants me to be like Him. Over the years, Phil and I have come a long way in our marriage. It is wonderful and solid and real. We don't have many arguments anymore, but it didn't start out like that.

The Gift Exchange

Next to conferences, some of the roughest touchdowns Phil and I had concerned holiday gift-giving. Oh boy, it took us a while to get that one greased on the runway. Christmas, especially, was always a setup for disaster as we tried to get just the right gift. Phil would give me a tool set for the house, or an ice maker, and I'd give him a mixer or a new tablecloth.

We have now worked out a rather smooth system for gifts: we each go buy our own. Then we bring it home and say, "Honey, look what you bought me!" This has vastly improved our taste. I do not know Phil's shopping formula, but I shop with a rhythm something like this: one for you, one for me, one for you and one for me. Christmas has never been so much fun, and the gifts are just perfect.

We have a little saying between us that has helped smooth our approach and landing. It is, "The appropriate response is..." I will never forget the time I came home with a new dress and asked Phil how he liked it. He said, "It looks comfortable." Comfortable? Comfortable? That was not the answer I was looking for. It was not even close. I never wore that dress again.

Now when I ask his opinion of my new outfit—before he can suck in a breath—I clue him in. "Phil, the appropriate response is, 'Honey, you have never looked better. You are stunning, and I think you look skinny in it.'" To which he replies, "You took the words right out of my mouth." What a man.

When he wants a new computer and I ask how much that will cost, his answer is, "Honey, the appropriate response is...'You worked for that money, you spend it any way you want.'" He took the words right out of my mouth.

Numbers, especially dollars, can give us so many problems in relationships. In aviation there are many terms that exist around "the numbers." When you make a better-than-average landing and roll out with runway to spare it is called "landing on the numbers." When you file a flight plan, some of the information is called "figuring the numbers." Numbers in regard to weight, winds and women are IMPORTANT. Phil can tell you how important numbers are to this woman.

Marital Mis-Adjustments

One summer we were going to rent a houseboat for our vacation. Phil decided to get his fishing license before we left, so I asked him to get me one too, so we could fish together. When he got home, he told me that in order to get the license, he had to tell them my weight. I clenched my teeth and said, "What did you say?"

Now Phil is a man who knows how to tread softly. He learned a long time ago to say I look great in anything from P.J.'s to pup tents. He also knew our whole trip depended on his answer. He said, "Honey, when that woman asked me your weight, I told her I wasn't going to touch that with a ten foot pole. When she insisted I had to give her some idea, I said somewhere between 100 and 200 pounds."

"Honey, you did gooooood."

The woman wrote "135 lbs." on the form, and I sent her a check.

Taking the Tribune

Once in a while I get a chance to talk to the "pilot" before Phil does. If things are not going smoothly, I take that opportunity to straighten out the situation. For instance, since Phil retired from air traffic control a few years ago and is home all the time, he buys lots of things over the phone. I mean, he will buy *anything* over the phone. We have at least thirty-two cemetery lots, thirty of which I'm planning to give away at my next seminar.

One day I came home and Phil said, "Honey, we're going to take home delivery on the Tampa Tribune."

"Why? Phil, we live *90 miles* from Tampa. Why would we take the Tampa Tribune?"

"It's on sale."

"Who cares? I can't get down there for the sales, I don't know anyone in the obituaries, and I don't know anyone in politics. Why would we do this?"

"It's on sale."

"Phil, please don't order the Tampa Tribune. "

About ten days later I was home alone when the phone rang.

"This is the Tampa Tribune," a young man said. "Bet you are wondering why you haven't been getting your paper."

"No, not really."

"We can't find your house."

"Let me tell you something: cancel this order."

"Wait a minute. Mr. Martin ordered the paper."

"I understand that. Cancel the order."

"May I speak to Mr. Martin?"

"Not a problem. But I need to tell you something before you do. Mr. Martin's brain is not what it used to be, and he'll order anything over the phone. If you think you can get a check out of him, go ahead and send the paper."

"Sorry I bothered you Mrs. Martin."

Phil Lies; I Exaggerate

Now I have to be honest. There is absolutely nothing wrong with Phil's mind—except that he doesn't always see things my way. I lied to that man in order to get things resolved to my satisfaction. I confess I sometimes have a problem with admitting and facing my sins, and I often live a double standard. In my book, Phil lies; I exaggerate. I am amazed at the lengths I go to polish my side of things. Phil's faults are sins, period. Mine are bad habits, poor judgment, mistakes, oversights and miscalculations. Never sin for me; no, that couldn't define me. Obviously it defines others, but not me.

When you see yourself and others in that light, you quite naturally feel called to help them out of the mess they are in. After all, sin can be quite a quagmire. You set your sights on adjusting others.

From time to time I hear the voice of the Lord say something that gets my attention, and I have to re-evaluate the approach I am taking to trying to smooth out the landings. Once the Lord said, "If I were as hard on you, as you are on others, God help you." We are so prone to see the need for adjustment in others and not ourselves.

In the first few years of our marriage, Phil and I were on that merry-go-round. I hadn't even shaken the rice out of my hair when I began to think, "What have I done? He does almost nothing right. My stars, why didn't I notice that before? We will have to do something about that right away." I would flee to my bedroom to pray for him. "Lord, I know you made Phil and you can change him."

I just knew I had been sent to Phil to help him adjust. Phil, on the other hand, was thinking the same thing about me. Gasp. He was also praying for the one who created me, to change me. Once in a while we would try to pray together. If we had argued, one of us would venture a simple suggestion. "Do you think we ought to pray about this?" The reply was usually, "Go ahead, you're the one who needs it." We have both been guilty of that. Or we would pray together, and barely touch fingers. Have you done that? We'd come out of the room and realize it hadn't worked, so we'd have to go back in and pray again.

Finally, after years of trying to get each other where we wanted them, we began to get the idea that maybe the formula was faulty. I can remember the day I was again praying for Phil to "get with it" when the Lord impressed on me, "Stop praying for Phil to change."

"What? He's my mission field. My ministry. My call."

"No, he is not. He's mine. I want you to begin to pray that you will be the kind of wife he needs. You see, Gaye, I want to use the same vessel to build him up, that tore him down."

Ouch.

I quit praying that God would change Phil, and started praying that He would change me.

Obviously, Phil and I had some difficulties between the two of us. But there were other cross-currents that threatened our landing safely. Figure out what happens when you factor in five children. Let's see, how do you spell chaos?

The Sunday Morning Shuffle

I don't know who said Sunday is a day of rest, but I want names, and I want to know if they had children. I can tell you that on Sunday mornings in our home, as soon as you opened your eyes, you had to say, "Today is the day which the Lord hath made. I will rejoice and be glad in it" (Psalm 118:24) And you'd better say it FAST, because it was downhill from then on.

We had this little rule in our home when the children were growing up. Because we all had to get ready to go to church, on Sunday mornings, you could either sleep late or Mom would do a big breakfast. The children almost always opted for sleeping late. That was fine with me. We'd all sleep late and then, just a little bit before we had to leave for church, they'd finally crawl out of bed and say, "Mom, let's do waffles."

"Wait. Time out. Remember, we slept late. Have some cereal."

"Cereal?" they whined. "We have cereal every morning."

"I know. But we don't have time for me to do waffles."

"Aw, Mom. It doesn't make any difference if we're a little late..."

I could just feel the anger and frustration welling up in me. Then my son would come out of his room in blue jeans with grass stains on them.

"Scott, you CANNOT wear that to church!"

"Mo-om, everyone else does."

"But you're not everyone else."

"I know that, Mother. Thanks to you, I'm a weirdo."

"You may be, but you're a clean one. Change your clothes."

Then Fran would come out in a skirt way up her thighs. "Fran, you are not wearing that to church."

"But the preacher's daughter—"

"The preacher's daughter is a hussy! And you're not...yet."

I'm trying to get all this together, and guess where old "prophet and priest" is during all this? Uh, huh. He's in the bedroom. Reading his devotions. Having a cup of coffee. And glancing at the newspaper.

In no time at all, prophet and priest is in the car, tooting the horn. I'm rounding up five kids. Throwing out two cats. I leave the house, and I don't even know if I am together. There were Sundays I had to stop and make sure I had a skirt on.

I'd get out in the car, so frazzled, and Phil would very calmly and deliberately say, "Honey, is there a *reason* why we can't be ready on time?"

My response would be, "YES!! There are ninety-three reasons! Someone had to get the kids up. Guess who? Someone had to fix breakfast. Guess who? Someone had to unplug the curling iron, and the iron, so the house doesn't burn down. Good thought, don't you think. Guess who? Someone had to put dinner on so we can eat when we get home. Guess who? "

He would respond, "Are you upset?"

"I'm not upset. What makes you think I'm upset?"

So there we are on the way to church, and we're not speaking to each other. You could cut the tension with a knife. Now, for years, we drove a Volkswagen bug. Try to draw a line down the back seat and keep five kids from touching each other.

There was one son, which I've told you about—tuxedo-tennis shoes—that would always pipe up on the way to church and say, "Are we eating out today?"

Child, you didn't do that in our family, because that *launched* Phil into a monologue about how lucky we were to eat out as often as we did And about how seldom he ate out as a child—which was apparent when he ate out. He would then tell us how many airplanes he had to control to buy us a taco.

I would look back at Steven and give him a glare that said, "You're dead meat."

Because, you see, Phil would then go on to tell us about how he walked to school uphill both ways in the snow, and it got longer and further and colder with every retelling.

Finally, we would arrive at church. We'd get out of the car and greet people with a smile and a handshake, saying, "Love you…" "Bless God…" "Good to see you…"

Have you had Sundays like that? We have the idea that if there is any hardship or failure in our lives, then we can't be the shining example of Sparky Spiritual we have determined to be—if it kills us. But the truth is, the scripture is full of warnings that we will be tried, tested, fired, molded, and formed.

I Peter 4:12-13 says,

Beloved, think it not strange concerning the fiery trial which is to try you, as though some strange things happened unto you. But rejoice, inasmuch as ye are partakers of Christ's sufferings that when his glory shall be revealed, ye may be glad also with exceeding joy.

Christ suffered; He understands that it is painful—but necessary to make us the people He designed us to be. His working in our lives is that of a blacksmith. To transform a metal rod into a useful tool, the rod must first be heated. Then the blacksmith carefully fashions it into the desired shape. Though underneath it is still the same metal, it has been changed into something valuable. It takes a very hot fire to make the metal pliable. Firing leads to form.

Christ is acquainted with the flame. He knows the way through the molding process and will make His appearance as we are fashioned into useful tools that fit His hand.

> Though he [Jesus] were a Son yet learned He obedience by the things which He suffered...For it became Him for whom are all things and by whom are all things, in bringing many sons unto glory, to make the captain of their salvation perfect through sufferings...If we suffer, we shall also reign with Him. If we deny Him He also will deny us...The disciple is not above his master, nor the servant above his Lord (Hebrews 5:8, Hebrews 2:10, 2 Tim. 2:12, Matthew 10:24).

There seems to be a necessary time of testing to determine our metal and our worth. My word, if time in the fire counts, Phil and I might be close to perfect. You have probably been "fired" a few times, too. It is painful, but remember, there is a purpose and design in it all.

Phil and I prayed for a long time for Jesus to make us "real." I got so tired of faking it, that if firing and testing will work it in me, I now say, "bring it on."

But, could I just simmer, and not boil? There I go again, trying to negotiate how it's done. Joyce Meyer talked about our willingness to sing "I Surrender All" until the Lord shows us something he wants to take out of our lives. Then we begin to hum, "I Surrender Some."

Sin Redefined

It amazes me how the Lord will speak the same message to our hearts in various ways in an attempt to help us learn the lesson He has prepared for us. God spoke to me before a retreat just a few months back and said, "The greatest tool, the greatest sin in the enemy's hand, is for you to make a strong declaration of your faith—like the bumper stickers and the pins—and then to live beneath it."

I must say that has caused me to do a lot of thinking. It reminded me of one of the most profound definitions of sin I have ever heard. If I am correct, I heard Dr. Ravi Zacharias of Atlanta relate this in one of his meetings. It is so direct and powerful that I have written it in every Bible I have as a reminder. It seems that as a young man, John Wesley asked Susannah Wesley, "Mother, what is sin?"

Her reply was this:

"Whatever weakens your reasoning;
whatever impairs the tenderness of your conscience;
whatever obscures your sense of God;
whatever takes away your relish for spiritual things;
whatever increases the power of the flesh over the spirit;
to you it is sin."

If we confess our sins [not mistakes, exaggerations oversights, etc.] He is faithful and just to forgive us our sins, and to cleanse us from all unrighteousness (I John 1:9).

Chapter Nine

If You're Flying in Circles—
Admit You're Lost

For most women, asking for directions is not that hard. But I have a terrible time admitting I'm lost. I think it stems from that "fake-it-till-you-make-it" attitude with which I struggle.

Some years ago I flew up from Miami to speak at some meetings in Atlanta. I knew exactly where I was as I came up through Florida. I knew exactly when I passed over Gainesville, and exactly when I passed over Lake City. I had paid attention, and was watching everything I did.

When I got into southern Georgia, I realized I would be landing soon. I decided to take just a few minutes—that's all it takes, a few minutes—to fix my face. I wanted to make a good first impression, so it was important that I look stunning when I got out of the airplane.

I did my face and my hair, and I guess it took longer than I thought it would. When I turned back to my flying, I didn't know where I was. I looked at the map. I looked at the ground. I looked back at the map and thought, *This is crazy.* I couldn't find the railroad tracks that ought to be there. I couldn't find *anything* that ought to be there.

I did know I was supposed to report in over Griffin, Georgia, a little town just south of Atlanta. I looked down, saw a little town and thought, *Well, I'll just fake it until I make it.* I called the tower in Atlanta and said, "This is 3440 Delta. I am over Griffin, Georgia. Landing in Atlanta."

After several moments of silence, the controller said, "3440 Delta, I don't have you on radar."

I thought, *Bless his heart. It's another new controller.*

I flew several more minutes until I saw another little town. I called the Atlanta center again. "This is 3440 Delta, reporting over Griffin, Georgia."

The same controller said, "You know what? I can't find you on radar."

I reported over Griffin, Georgia, four times. I don't know what little towns I was passing over, but I reported over every one of them. Finally he said to me, "3440 Delta, do you see a green water tower? That's in Griffin, Georgia."

"No, sir, I don't."

"Do you see a raceway? That would be the Atlanta raceway."

I said again, "No sir, I don't."

"3440 Delta, do you see Stone Mountain?"

"Yes, sir, I do!"

"Here's what you need to do. I want you to do a 360 degree turn so I can identify you on the radar."

Do you know how uncool it is, when every other airplane is flying in a straight line, and you're doing circles? That's just not cool.

He said, "Are you lost?"

"No, sir."

As soon as I started making circles he said, "I've got you." Then he said, "Listen to me. Trust me. Follow my directions and I'll get you back on course."

He gave me a couple of turns, and next thing I knew, I was lined up with the runway in Atlanta. After I landed he said, "3440 Delta, any time I assist a pilot, I need to file a report. Would it be safe to say that you were 'temporarily disoriented'?"

"I can live with 'lost.'"

When I got on the ground, I went to the tower and talked to that man. "I want to thank you for your help, and for reaching out and getting me back on track."

Do you know what he said to me? "It's my pleasure. It's my job."

Don't be afraid to admit when you're lost—or to ask for help. I've found God will sometimes allow things to spin out of our control to remind us that, left to our own devices, we get off course very easily. He also needs to bring us to the place where we can admit we are lost. If you are like me, you will muddle about for quite some time before you admit you don't have a clue where you are—or how to get from here to where you want to be. Remember that God can't help you if you can't admit you need help.

I will never forget that controller's final words. They remind me of the verse in Luke 12:32 where Jesus tells us "Fear not little flock, for it is your Father's good pleasure to give you the Kingdom."

Finding Yourself

Of course, if there is anything harder than keeping yourself on the right track, it's trying to get your children heading the same direction. It seems anything you value, they veto. Makes you wonder, if we wore the ponytail, would they get the flat top? If we played rock music till the rafters shook, would they embrace Bach? I don't have the courage to try it, do you?

Once in a while, I'll have a young man or woman just getting out of high school in one of my college classes. Generally, my students are somewhat older adults. I'll ask that graduate, "Matthew, you graduated from high school. Good for you. What do you want to do?"

"I don't know. Go to Daytona?"

"No, Matthew. I mean what do you want to DO?"

"Oh. I don't know."

"Well what do you think you'll need so you will know?"

"Time."

"Time?"

Isn't it amazing how today's youth feel they need time to find themselves. And they have to go to Arizona to whitewater raft—on my credit card—to find themselves. I found myself on the outskirts of Gainesville, Florida. That's as far as my folks could send me. These young people will say to me, "I just need to get away and peel away all these socially prescribed identities, and get down to the real me." To me, the obvious question is, "What if you peel, and nobody's home?"

We have five children, and every year we jokingly say to three of them, "Don't peel. It's not a good year to peel."

For some people, peel is all there is. But ladies and gentlemen, I want to tell you that you don't *find* your identity. It isn't lost. Your identity is *created* in Jesus Christ. He gives you your identity. We don't have one apart from Jesus.

Learning to take His word for it, and believing in our identity and position in Christ is not always easy. Our perceptions get scrambled and we're not sure if we are seeing ourselves clearly or not. We think we might be heading in the right direction, but we're not sure.

It is similar to night landings. These are the last ones you are trained in—and the hardest to master. Night landings are so difficult because your depth perception is not as acute then as it is in the daytime. When you line up for the final approach toward a lighted runway, it is very difficult to determine exactly where the surface of the runway is. From the air it looks like a ditch, and not a hard surface. Therefore, you must gauge carefully—so you don't fly straight into it. Perception can play havoc in life if you are not fully aware of your position.

The Power of Perceptions

For example, take Toni, one of my students at the college. Toni is anorexic—and no bigger than a minute—but she is the neatest girl I've ever met. I love to talk to Toni; and since she has had so much therapy, an hour with her is like a free session.

One day I said, "Toni, do you know that you and I are afflicted with the same disease?" I know what went through her mind at that point. She looked at me thinking, "If you are healed, I don't want to go there."

"Oh really," she said. "How do you see that?"

"When you look in the mirror, what do you see?"

"Fat."

"Now when I look in the mirror, I think *Whoa. Not bad*."

We're both sick. But it's a sickness of perception.

More than one pilot has had the perception that he could maneuver around a storm, and so has ignored the warnings—only to find himself on the side of a mountain. He didn't think he was lost, or needed help. Some have walked away from crashes like that, but most do not. Unfortunately, when we ignore the warnings of others, we often injure not just ourselves, but those all around us.

Shining a Light for Others

I was invited to speak at a candlelight service on the town square in Ocala, honoring domestic violence victims in our community. We planned to light a candle for each life lost in our area as a result of domestic violence. As soon as it got dark, the candles would be blown out.

I address domestic violence in some of the classes I teach, but I learned about it in another arena altogether. In my first marriage, my children and I were victims of domestic violence. When I accepted the invitation to speak, I felt I had come full circle. I am a survivor and I want to let women know it is possible to survive, to move past it, and it is even possible for God to use that tragedy in your life.

I arrived early so I could see the T-shirts hung on clotheslines around the block. Part of the therapy for the women and children trying to re-build their lives is to design a T-shirt. There must have been 150 shirts hanging there, all with messages wrung from sad experiences.

Right after I arrived, a young lady of about eight years old came up to me and latched onto me, as children always do. (I think it's because I'm fluffy.) She told me her name was Carol, and I could see in her this appetite for kindness and care.

"Carol, do you have a T-shirt here?"

"Oh, yes. I had so many bad 'speriences, I got to do three T-shirts."

"Please let Miss Gaye know when we get to one of your T-shirts."

Several minutes later we stopped to admire the first of her shirts. Part of it said, "Pray."

"Carol, do you pray?"

"Um, hmm."

"And do you pray every day?"

"Oh, yes."

"I pray every day, too." Right then, Carol and I promised to pray for each other every day. Later, she stood right next to me—I mean right up close against me—in the gazebo while I spoke. Afterwards, she said, "Miss Gaye, I have a great idea. You take my candle, and I'll take your candle to remind us to pray for each other."

I still have her candle, and I don't ever see it that I don't pray for Carol. You see, Carol could easily have been one of my children at one time. She is one of my children at one time.

As I looked at those T-shirts, I wrote down the sayings on six of them, and I want to share them with you. The first one was done by the cutest eight-year-old boy you have ever seen in your life. I'd hate to be his Dad, because this little boy signed his shirt. His father had shot and killed his mother. On his T-shirt, the boy had drawn a big heart. Then he had twisted a little piece in the middle of the heart and cut it out, so there was a hole. Under it he'd written, "This is the hole in my heart where my Mommy used to live."

Another shirt said, "Dad, when you stole my body, you stole my soul."

One had a worm in an apple, and it said, "You got a lot of me, but you didn't get all of me."

Still another had a picture of a little stick-figure girl on a bed with a picture of hands all around the bed that said simply, "Hands hurt."

Another one had a big face with a wide-open mouth that said, "Life is a scream."

But there was one T-shirt, done by an adult, that just shattered me when I saw it. It had "Helpless" written across the top of it, and under that there was an upside-down church with the words, "No sanctuary for me here."

My first thought was, "Oh Lord, please don't let that be my church." You don't know who people come in contact with, and you don't know how they are treated.

That shirt reminds me to be so very careful about how I respond to hurting people. When we see someone who needs help, do we slam the door in their face? If Christians won't help those who've lost their way in life, who will?

God Sees Us Where We Are

The other reason that T-shirt hit so close to home is that I was once in dire need of a word of encouragement and hope. But my story is different from this woman's, because through some church people, God bent low and spoke healing to my heart.

It was about 30 years ago, and my marriage was crumbling around me. I had not shared it with anyone, but I was going through the collapse of a home, and I was grieved, so grieved in my spirit.

One night I was teaching a Bible study in a small church, and in the middle of what I was saying, a lady walked down the aisle and stood in front of me. I stopped talking and just looked at her. Finally I asked, "May I help you?"

She said, "God has a word for you." What kind of courage does that take? "God wants me to tell you that He has seen what the canker worm has eaten away in your life. He will restore it to you sevenfold, and He will confirm His word to you before sundown tomorrow."

I can tell you that's only happened to me once. I thanked her profusely and then began to cry, because I knew the "canker worm" was eating a lot away from my life and my family's life. I cannot imagine the courage it took for her to say those things to a complete stranger.

By the next morning I was in an altogether different city. I picked up a friend of mine on the way to another speaking engagement. We were traveling up I-95, and I was chatting away, when she suddenly got very quiet.

"You're not listening to me."

My friend had not been in the meeting the night before, and I had not told her about what happened. She finally said, "Gaye, I think God wants me to tell you something. He wants you to know that He sees what the canker worm has eaten from you, and He's going to restore it to you sevenfold. I think this is a confirmation."

I couldn't believe it. During the darkest period of my life, God let me know He had not forgotten me. I did not know where I was in life or where I was going, but He did. Through those two women, He gave me something solid to hold onto. When I felt the ground of my life crumbling under me, God gave me a toehold: the assurance of His presence. It reminded me of the mountain climbers I watch on the nature channel. As they climb straight up a flat rock face, first they look for a toehold, then a foothold, and finally, they have a strong hold. When they gain even an inch of new ground, they tenaciously defend it until they find another place that offers an opportunity to take more ground.

Like the controller in his tower, God always sees us right where we are. And like the controller, when we get lost, or we need a toehold, He is there to get us back on solid footing.

Ask Him. He'll help.

"It's my pleasure. It's my job."

Chapter Ten

When Visibility is Zero, Trust the One with the Whole Picture

Pilots often describe flying as serene routine punctuated by stark terror. An apt description of life too, don't you think? Sometimes serene erupts into serious faster than you can wrap your mind around. In the blink of an eye, clear skies turn to howling wind and freezing rain, visibility drops to nil—and you must rely on the unseen controller to get you through safely. As a new pilot, I wrongly assumed that if I couldn't see danger from the cockpit, it didn't exist.

On a trip to Wilmington, Delaware, however, I became acutely aware that my visual field was not the whole picture. Before I left Miami that day, I pre-planned the trip. I knew all the headings I had to fly, and had figured in the winds. I knew the route to Wilmington was by way of Charlotte, knew how long it would take to get there, and how long it would take to re-fuel.

I was feeling pretty confident when I got into Charlotte right on the money. After I re-fueled and got ready to take off, the air traffic controller said, "3440Delta, I want you to fly the heading I assign you until I terminate service." Since I was in his jurisdiction, I had no choice but to comply. Do you know he assigned me a *due east* heading? You don't have to be a rocket scientist to realize you can't get to Wilmington that way.

Still, I flew due east. I flew, and flew, and flew. Then I began to wonder what the problem was. I decided he must be a new controller, and he'd forgotten me. Since I had to get to Wilmington *that week*, I began to deviate just slightly from that due east course.

I had not gone a quarter of an inch when I heard that controller say, "3440 Delta, do you have a problem?"

"Negative."

"Then why is it your heading doesn't coincide with the one I assigned you?"

I know you wouldn't have done this, and I don't know why I did, but I said, "Well, to be honest with you, I thought possibly...well, I thought maybe you didn't know my destination."

"Wilmington, Delaware."

Aw, he got that right. Then I said, "Seriously, I thought you had forgotten me."

"3440 Delta, I have not forgotten you. However, if you continue on the course you are currently flying, you are going to come in very close contact with commercial traffic in the form of a United Airlines 747—and one or both of you will make an unscheduled stop over the water."

"Roger. I'm leaving my current heading for the assigned one."

I heard him say, "Excellent choice."

That experience taught me to trust the one with the larger picture. What I felt was misdirection and unnecessary delay was in reality the controller vectoring me around imminent danger—danger he saw, and I could not. Comforting, isn't it? We learn our Heavenly Father does exactly that when storms begin to encroach on our lives and determine to blow us off course. Surviving a recent tornado confirmed how far-reaching the controller's care really is.

The Wind is a' Blowin

I was home with our granddaughter, Stephanie, while Phil was in Maryland, when a tornado hit our little town on January 7, 1996. When people in our area tell me they heard about it, I ask, "Where were you when I was plastered to the pine tree? I don't remember seeing you coming and trying to get me out."

As a native Floridian, I knew a lot about hurricanes, but very little about tornadoes. I know a bit more about them now, though, than I did then. I know you have to be on a first name basis with God when they hit, because you don't have time to get right with Him. You don't have time for a long prayer. You barely have time to say, "Dear God!"

I woke up at 5:30 in the morning and didn't know what I was hearing. I thought there was hail hitting the windows, but it wasn't. It turned out to be my next door neighbor's furniture. To be honest, I sort of wish now that I had opened my windows about the time her china came through.

Thunder boomed, lightning flashed and the wind started howling. I didn't have but a minute, so I snatched Stephanie out of bed, and we huddled in the hallway, because I didn't know what else to do. I wasn't particularly concerned about getting sucked *out* of the hallway because I have to grease my hips to get *into* the hallway, but I was a bit concerned about Stephanie. I hung on to her and we crouched in the hallway as this thing went over.

Stephanie, who was ten at the time, has always been afraid of thunderstorms. I have always said, "Stephanie, you don't need to be afraid of thunderstorms, Sugar. Because when it rains, it means God's washing his windows and when it thunders, it means God's moving his furniture."

Suddenly there was a loud clap of thunder and a tree hit the house. Stephanie grabbed hold of my jammies and screamed, "Nanie! I think God dropped his couch!"

Finally the tornado passed over, but it was still pitch dark. When lightning flashed and I could peek out the windows, nothing on my horizon looked familiar. Absolutely nothing. I said to Stephanie, "You know, if indeed we still have a telephone, I need to call your Mom and let her know we're okay, and I need to call Papa in Maryland and let him know that I'm okay."

We called Phil in Maryland at 5:45 in the morning. "Honey, we have just been through a tornado."

Now Phil is so male. Would you like to know what he said? "Calm down, Honey. Calm down. Are you SURE it was a tornado?"

"Read my lips!"

"Calm down, Honey," he said again. "What makes you THINK it was a tornado?"

"Well, Phil, there's a tree down on the car, a tree down on the van, and four trees down on the house. There's a ceiling fan, a commode, and a *whole* lot of pots and pans that don't belong to us in the side yard. Now that could be a clue. Then of course the people who lived two streets behind us are now our next door neighbors. And do you remember the boat that was tied up at the dock? It's wedged in a tree." I took a deep breath and said, "Phil, you need to know I almost went to heaven in pink polka-dot pajamas and a blue canoe."

By the way, I don't look like much during the day, but since January 7, you should see me when I go to bed at night. I mean, I am stunning. When you ladies are taking your makeup off, I'm putting mine on. I look like a hussy. I am not going to heaven in pink polka-dot pajamas. I almost did.

Phil has said to me since then, "Honey...I kinda wish this tornado had hit earlier..."

And I always say, "Listen, don't touch me. This outfit is for God."

But back to that first call to Phil. I finally said, "Phil, your boat is flat."

That got through. "Golly, Honey, it might have been a tornado."

Even then, God knew. He saw us, and He took care of us. In the middle of that storm, when the things right outside our window looked foreign to us, God was there. It is so vital that we trust God, even when we can't see the future. Sometimes we can't see beyond the next few hours, but He can. If we put ourselves in the hands of the controller, the winds may blow, the ride might get rough, but the landing will be safe. In fact, the GOAL of the controller is to keep you advised of threatening weather and help you touch down safely. True training for a "real" pilot is to learn to listen to an unseen voice and to trust that voice. One of my favorite old stories illustrates this so well.

A Child-Like Faith—At Any Age

There was a church that had testimony time every Sunday. Every week the same little old lady would stand up and say, "God supplies every bite of food that goes in my mouth, and He sends it supernaturally."

One day several teenage boys decided to play a trick on her. They bought a bag of potatoes, and then went to her house, climbed up on the roof and listened while she prayed for her evening meal. When she finished, they dropped the potatoes down the chimney, one by one. After each one fell they heard her say, "Praise God. Thank you, God, for my evening meal."

When they were done, the boys climbed down from the roof and knocked on her front door. "Boys, boys, come in. God has sent my evening meal."

"God didn't send that," they said. "We bought those potatoes and we've been dropping them down the chimney."

"Boys," she said, "the devil may have *brought* that meal, but God *sent* it."

Isn't God wonderful!   He is in charge, whether others believe it or not. Oh, for a relationship with the controller where I can put His face on every blessing and every test. We are prone to credit or blame the face in front of us, and not understand the source of our supply.

Chart-Snooping at the Doctor's Office

While I greatly admire that little old lady's faith, I admit I am still curious. I want to be on the inside track—especially when it comes to future events. I don't know about you, but when I go into the doctor's office and he leaves the room, I look through my chart. I can't stand not looking. I don't know why I do that, or even what I'm looking for. I guess I just want to see what he writes about me. Once I skimmed through my chart looking for words like "stunning" or "gorgeous," or "life expectancy: 100" but they weren't there. When the doctor came in, only one word on my chart had registered with me, just one. "Obese!"

I said, "Dr. H., give me a break."

"What are you talking about?"

"Obese? Please. What's wrong with 'fluffy?' What's wrong with 'substantial?' What is wrong with 'Renaissance Woman?'"

He narrowed his eyes and said, "You've been looking at your chart."

"I have."

"Well, be thankful I haven't put 'morbidly' in front of the word 'obese' yet."

It is hard when you don't know the future or the plans. Sometimes we even wonder if God has gone on vacation. Have you ever felt He had completely forgotten you? I felt like that when Phil was transferred to Hilliard, Florida. Does anybody know where Hilliard is? I wasn't sure God knew where Hilliard, Florida, is, so I marked it on a map for Him.

But God *does* know the plans. There is great comfort and strength to be gained alone with Him.

As a child of God, I prepare for this trip called life by spending time alone with my Heavenly Father, and studying His word. As a pilot I learned that the flight plan is my preparation for the trip. It lets me calculate the miles, the winds, the fuel, and alternate airports—should I need them. It gives me a handle on the estimated course and time of arrival. It is easy to expect the trip to evolve *exactly* like I had it on the flight plan. Unfortunately, that's not always the case.

On the other hand, the plans of our Heavenly Father are not changeable. He makes that clear in Jeremiah 29:11 (NIV). There He tells us of His plan… "For I know the plans I have for you," declares the Lord, "plans to prosper you and not to harm you, plans to give you hope and a future." That scripture should speak to our curiosity in regard to the inside scoop on future events, and fill us with the knowledge we have indeed looked over his shoulder and seen the inside track. Sight unseen, He is still the choreographer of all our paths.

You Dyin' Nanie!

However, I'll never again complain about what I get for Christmas. When Phil and I first married, he gave me a rod and reel for Christmas, so the next year I gave him a night gown. Another year he gave me a treadmill. Now that is a fun gift. Even today it only has seven miles on it; six of those are me saying, "Honey, show me again how this works." It has three settings: warm up, fat burn, and aerobic. It should have read: Cardiac arrest, call 911, and you're going to meet Jesus today.

But if you think those are bad gifts, several Christmas Eve's ago I found a lump in my breast. Let me tell you, jingle bells, jingle bells. I was so nervous when I went to the doctor that I said, "I found a breast on my lump." That's the kind of nervous women can understand.

Within no time at all they had sent me to the hospital and run some tests. I found out the lump was malignant, but because it was over the Christmas holidays, my surgeon was on vacation. I wanted to call him at home and say, "Scrub. Meet me at Waffle House. Because this has got to come out."

I will never forget coming out of the treatment room after the ultrasound. The doctor looked at me and said, "It does not look good. It does not look good."

My daughter, Fran, and granddaughter, Stephanie, had gone with me, so when we got outside I said, "Fran, let me take you to breakfast to thank you for going with me and supporting me in this."

Stephanie piped up with, "Well, wait a minute, Nanie, we'll pay. Cause you dying."

"I don't think I'm dying *today*, Steph."

As soon as they scheduled my surgery, I started praying my lymph nodes weighed five pounds apiece, so I could lose fifty pounds. No such luck. It seems I have "petite" lymph nodes. I woke up just a week or so later with several incisions and a lot of staples. Five days after my surgery, I taught Sunday School, and I have to tell you, when you have staples, hugging people is like a religious experience. You can almost get saved doing that. You just pray it doesn't rain, so you don't rust. I told Phil my new fragrance of choice was WD40, and he got *so* attentive. I mean, he got *really* attentive. I guess it's because I smelled like his shop.

After the surgery, I had to have 34 radiation treatments. I *was* the glow on your horizon. I also got this wonderful tan nobody wanted to see, but I'm fine now. I still want them to mammogram the other breast every Friday, but I'm told that's normal. Still, I would like to open a drive-through mammogram center: "I want a cheeseburger, a chocolate shake, and a mammogram to go." Or, a mammo-van that comes to my neighborhood...

But beyond the surgery and radiation, I went through some other things when this happened. I had to come into a place with the Lord where we talked seriously about my place in His plan. Not His place in *my* plan, my place in *His*. He had allowed things to spin out of my control, so I had to say to Him, "Jesus, I don't know if it's your time to call me home or not. I don't know."

I made my requests known to the Lord, because Philippians 4:6 tells me I can do that. It says, "Do not be anxious about anything, but in everything, by prayer and petition, with thanksgiving, present your requests to God" (NIV). I said to the Lord, "I want very much to be around at least as long as my parents are, because they took care of me when my first marriage fell apart. It's really important to me to be there when they need me, and they need me. I want more years with Phil, and I want more years with my children and grandchildren. But it is in your hands, Lord. It was written on your calendar long before I entered the world."

I also realized something else I had not thought of before. I had to say, "Jesus I do not have one thing I can bring to you. Nothing. All I have is the blood of Jesus." I had to confess to the Lord that everything I have ever done has had a personal agenda attached to it. Everything. I had to admit that, and repent of it. Even if, once in a while, I slipped up and did something altruistic and benevolent—without a personal agenda—it would only be an hour or so until I was proud of it. So I said to the Lord, "You know, and I know—and you know me better than anyone else does—that if the blood of Jesus is not enough, then I can't come to heaven."

But it is enough.

It is during these emergencies that we get enormous insight into how limited we are and how powerful He is. No doubt about it, fear knocks first, but then all the training and all the instruction, all the teaching and all the prayer kick in. They take the reins and harness fear.

"Be anxious for NOTHING, but in EVERYTHING by prayer and supplication, with thanksgiving let your requests be made known to God. And the peace of God which surpasses all understanding will guard your hearts and minds through Christ Jesus" (Philippians 4:6-7, emphasis mine).

Life's Seas

Just as every pilot will encounter rough weather at times, every child of God will encounter some rough seas. Child, sometimes they are not just storms, they are tidal waves (or tornadoes). Yet God promises to go with us. The Psalms have encouraging words for us when life's seas get rough:

"Listen, everyone! High and low, rich and poor, all around the world—listen to My words, for they are wise and filled with insight. I will tell in song accompanied by harps the answer to one of life's most perplexing problems: *There is no need to fear when times of trouble come*, even though surrounded by enemies!" (Psalm 49:1-5 TLB).

"What I want from you is your true thanks; I want your promises fulfilled. *I want you to trust me in your times of trouble, so I can rescue you, and you can give me glory*" (Psalm 50:14-15 TLB).

"But when I am afraid, I will put my confidence in you. Yes, I will trust the promises of God. And since I am trusting him, what can mere man do to me?

"You have seen me tossing and turning through the night. You have collected all my tears and preserved them in your bottle! You have recorded every one in your book. The very day I call for help, the tide of battle turns. My enemies flee. This one thing I *know*: *God is for me*. I am trusting God—oh, praise his promises! I am not afraid of anything mere man can do to me! Yes, praise his promises. I will surely do what I have promised, Lord, and thank you for your help (Psalm 56:8-12 TLB)."

Life's stormy seas are master instructors. They will test your mettle and your grit. They will reveal the height and the depth of you. They will force you to define your anchors, the ones that hold true. Their winds will drive you to new horizons of experience and endurance. They will also drive you to your knees and make you reach for God's hand.

Life's seas will expose you to opportunities to play fair, or not. They will introduce you to yourself, and with the right attitude and the right standard, you'll like what you see. At the end of the trip, when your sails are folded, you can step up on the dock and say, "Wow. What a trip!"

When it storms—and it will—and when everything is black, and nothing on your horizon is the least bit familiar, trust Him. Whether on the ground or in the air, He not only has you in His sights; He has you in His care.

Part III
Chapters Eleven - Fifteen

**Getting Our Wings—
The Rewards of
Listening**

Chapter Eleven

Holding Patterns Are No Fun, But the Alternative is Worse

Not long ago I spoke in a little church outside Birmingham, Alabama, over spring break. On the flight home I realized I was the oldest woman on that plane. Everyone else was younger, thinner, tanner and cuter than I was. I had plenty of time to figure this out because we sat on the runway for what seemed like hours before take-off. We were waiting for some weather to clear, or so we were told. Halfway home we hit that bad weather—and it was Big Time bad weather. That plane went up and down faster than any roller coaster I have ever been on.

Everyone got so quiet. I grabbed my Bible and went from Genesis to the maps at the back in three minutes flat. I claimed everything I knew—and repented of some things I have known about for a very long time. I got right with God.

Then I thought, *if this weather gets any worse, there is a very good possibility Phil is going to be identifying body parts*. So I began to pray, "God, please, let my head roll up next to a size 8 body, preferably one without a tattoo." You know, that would be a blessing for Phil. I can just see him saying, "Yup, that's her."

It crossed my mind I might not make it. Then you begin to think differently. That day I prayed for God to keep us in the air. There have been other times, though, when I wanted nothing more than to stay comfortably on the ground—when the Lord wanted me to take to the skies.

Sitting, When I Should Be Soaring

A professor from Asbury College once visited a farmer friend who lived in the woods. This farmer had a little over five acres of land, and it was swarming with mallard ducks. The professor asked, "How did you come by all these mallard ducks?" The farmer said, "Well, I found three eggs in the woods. I brought them home and put them under a bantam hen." You know bantam hens will sit on doorknobs. "And," he said, "they hatched out—two ladies and a gentlemen. They in turn attracted other wild ducks to the lake, and I now have a very sizable flock. However, this fall they saw other ducks on the wing, and became nervous, excited and agitated. I realized a time clock had gone off in their little duck hearts, and they were ready to defy gravity. But I didn't want to lose them, so you know what I did? I fed them an abundance of corn every day. They became so satisfied and so comfortable that the whole flock forgot to migrate."

The farmer seemed rather proud of that.

The professor said later, "Do you know what happened to those ducks? They stifled the urge to soar. They denied the upward call. They didn't respond promptly to the tug calling them to higher places. Therefore, they never did achieve their assigned destiny, and what they were created for. Instead of becoming *soaring ducks*, they became *sitting ducks*."

What a description of what happens when we fail to listen to the upward call of the Spirit in our lives. We get the burden to soar to new heights and immediately trot out all the reasons we aren't qualified or able to accept the call. The timing is wrong, we say, or maybe next summer…as soon as the kids are out of school…right after the cantata…after the holidays, and on it goes. You have to say good-bye to all of that in order to say hello to new places—and that is difficult to do.

Besides, who wants to be stuck in what was, when you can be soaring in what is? God is on the move—you can feel it. He is riding on the wind of new anointing and power. He is calling us to join Him as He marches through the earth in these last days. We are a people called to heavenly places and to be comfortable there.

To be honest, you can't hear the direction for your life while on the run. It is necessary to wait on His clearance. We tried to instill in our children the need not only to hear and heed our voice, but to hear and heed the voice of the Lord in their lives. That is no easy task, and we used various methods to accomplish that goal. One of them was that *dreadful* idea...

Family Devotions

Have you ever tried family devotions? Are they the pits, the absolute pits? They were the hardest thing we ever did in our home. I am so glad that's over. We tried every way we knew. We tried in the mornings, and we tried at night. We tried the Daily Bread. No matter what we did, family devotions were chaos. Frustrated, I said to the Lord, "How you can be a part of this, I don't know."

At one point, we had family devotions late in the afternoon, before everyone got busy at night or went to work. We'd have them with those that were home, and hopefully we hit everybody now and then. On this particular day, Phil was at work and I just had two boys at home. Scott was getting ready to go on a date, and Steven was going to stay home, because he was few years younger than Scott.

"Scott," I said, "before you go, let's just have family devotions. It's not going to be long, okay?" Some days, I'd pick just one verse. Most days, though, I would have one of the children pick a chapter, and then we'd divide it up and each read a section. Then I would ask, "What was your favorite verse?" I usually got answers like, "Two." So I would ask, "Why?" "Cause its short." Our kids weren't very spiritual.

They weren't very smart either, let me tell you. Out of five children—and I'm an educator—not once did a teacher send home a bumper sticker that said, "My child is an honor student at ...." No, we were the guys in the Walmart parking lot peeling them off your car, and putting them on ours. That's what happened to your bumper sticker.

There we were, trying to have devotions, when Steven said, "Let's do the 132nd Psalm." That was fine with me, and it's not that long. Scott read a few verses, and Steven interrupted every five words. "That's not the way you say that. Say it right."

Then while Steven read, Scott kept saying, "C'mon Steven. Hurry up. You know I'm supposed to go out tonight." Naturally, Steven read slower and slower. Steven always did hold his halo on with his horns.

As I listened to them I thought, "God, why do I bother? Why? How do I get through all this?"

We finished the 132nd Psalm, and Steven said, "Mom, could we read just one more?" Now he is just not that spiritual. He is that mean.

Scott groaned, "Aw c'mon, Steven, you know I have to go out."

I looked down and saw that the 133rd Psalm only has three verses in it. So I said, "Scott, let's just read the next one." Would you like to know what the 133rd Psalm says? "Behold, how good and pleasant it is for brothers to dwell together in unity."

My kids know John 3:16 and Psalm 133:1. The Lord has shown me He can overshadow enormous chaos.

Unfortunately, in the midst of chaos you are often tempted to think and say more than you intended. During a few crises in the airplane I was far more vocal about my thoughts than necessary. It didn't take me long to learn that giving voice to what was creeping around in my mind was to give it life. That truth is powerful. If your thoughts are positive, kind and generous, to express them can act as a blast of life in the current situation. It is mind-boggling to get a glimpse into the power of our thoughts and words.

"You're Free To Think It, Not Say It"

When we reprimanded our children, I could see the anger all over their faces. The old cliché "if looks could kill, I'd be dead" fit on more than one occasion. I knew by looking in their eyes that they were thinking things like, "I wish Donna's mother was my mother." My response was, "It's okay, so do I. I already called to see if she wants to trade, and she is not interested."

Of course, they thought of other, more creative, things than that, hence the following rule in our house. At the first sign of conflict Phil or I would say, "Go to your room and cool off. You are free to think those thoughts, but you're not free to say them."

That was an effective form of discipline until they were in their teens. At that point the Lord spoke to me in prayer one day. "Don't tell them that anymore. From now on, tell the children 'you are not allowed to say those angry thoughts out loud. You are not allowed to think them either.'" I knew we were moving to a new level of the Lord's control of their lives, and mine.

From then on we said, "You need to go in your bedroom and get delivered from what you are thinking about me." There were also times I had to confess to the children, "I need to go in my room and get delivered from what I am thinking about you right now." It was an early exercise in bringing every thought into captivity to the obedience of Christ.

Restraining negative thoughts is not the only way to learn to live with some sense of harmony and peace. They say far more is learned by example than by lecture. I once had a rather reserved flight instructor. He would answer all my questions, but he didn't just chit chat. I realized early on that when he did say something, it was important. One day I was complaining about my inability to grasp all the technical terms and master the assigned maneuvers. After about an hour, he announced that we best go back and try again another day.

"Why?" I asked. "Are you giving up on me?"

"No, but you are about as cheerful as a basket full of snakes today, and I don't fly with snakes." I adjusted my attitude with him from then on. He had painted a word picture that still flashes into my mind when someone shakes my cage. Our lives are full of those positioned along the path to assist us to a successful and seamless transition from fleshly to spiritual. The process, though, takes time.

If You Rush the Process, You Cloud the Product

Whenever I see boysenberry syrup in a grocery store or candy shop, it reaches out and carries me back to my Grandmother's house, where you could tell the day of the week by Grandma's activities. Monday through Friday chores were her way of targeting the weekend, when she welcomed and fed the endless family gathered around her dining room table.

Each room in her house had a magical ability to fling you to unexplored lands. The three-way mirror in her guest bedroom drew me for hours into its tunnel of reflected images. Her kitchen, though, had the power to awaken all your senses. Pot roast, potatoes and spiced peaches—with enough gravy to float the rolls and make serious stains on the tablecloth. It was as pleasurable to anticipate one of her meals as to indulge in them.

Grandma also took enormous pride in her jellies, clear evidence that it is possible to mine exquisite jewels from the simplest of fruit. On completion, each batch would stand in her kitchen windows for a few days, transforming it into a stained glass cathedral when the sun shone in. It was as though God was blessing the harvest of her hands. Any special occasion—a wedding, new baby, or unexpected guests—would send her scurrying to the pantry for a jar of her jeweled brew.

Not many knew the secret to the flawless gift, but those of us that played in her hallway knew. We had learned the hard way.

On jelly day she would cook the day's batch of fruit, usually apples. Then she would add boysenberries to the portion she had reserved for gifts. In her mind, that ingredient elevated the average to the luxurious and made it worth giving away.

After cooking the fruit, she would tie it in a cheese cloth bag and hang it on a doorknob to s-l-o-w-l-y drip into a pan beneath it. Ruby raindrops came from that bulging bag of hot fruit and berries. Knowing our temptation, she would say, "Don't squeeze the bag."

Don't squeeze the bag? Did she know how hard it was not to milk that bag of all its sticky sweetness? We would play closer and closer. How do I know it was sticky? I have disobeyed orders and "squeezed the bag." I have even stood sentry while a cousin or brother squeezed it.

Grandma always knew when the deed was done, even though she may have been in the yard hanging clothes or chatting with friends on the porch. With one glance she would assess the damage and would call us in. "Who squeezed the bag?"

How did she know? We had only squeezed a little. What was the big deal anyway? One day I asked her why that was such a rigid rule. Her answer? "If you try to rush the process, you cloud the product."

She has been gone since I was ten, and today her kitchen lessons are far more profound in my heart than they were then. I now know that Jesus is the boysenberry in my life. He is the ingredient that changes a very average person into a child of God. A child that when His work is completed will have the ability to make a contribution, to be given away. How we struggle with that process and how we try to rush it at times. If Grandma were here she would remind us, "If you try to rush the process, you cloud the product."

Time in the holding pattern is a very real part of almost any journey by air. It is designed as a tool for separating infringing traffic. It is also a tool used to help you fall into the pattern of traffic flow set up by the controller. He will often hold you for quite some time—until weather clears, or traffic diminishes. It is His way of safely processing your trip. To rush that process is to court danger, indeed. Much more important than my getting my way with God, is God getting His way with me.

Chapter Twelve

Fly High; Pray Hard

Imagine setting out on a months-long journey—and not arriving until forty years later. That is exactly what happened to the children of Israel. Because of their disobedience and lack of trust, God let them wander around for forty years. Had they put faith into practice and relied on God's leading, they would have gotten to the Promised Land many, many years sooner. Have you ever wandered in your own wilderness because of a fear of new places or a lack of faith in God's leadership?

While flying supplies to missionaries, Phil and I discovered that taking to the skies shortens the trip. Missionary friends of ours were stationed on the Cacatah River in the jungles of Columbia. There we learned the value of the airplane to the jungle and its people. Before the plane arrived, the trip to the nearest town took eleven days—in a dugout canoe. By air, the trip took just twenty minutes. Many a native Colombian swallowed his fear of flying in order to get to town and back in one day, instead of twenty-two. That is some leap over the jungle!

Once, when the regular pilot was ill, he asked me to fly and let him take the co-pilot's seat. Our passengers were a plane-load of Colombian men. They got on board excited about the trip—until they saw a woman climb into the pilot's seat. "Sister Gaye is the piloto?" they asked in unison. "Si, Si, senors" we replied. It got very quiet as we took off, and stayed quiet throughout the flight.

Wouldn't you know, just as we landed on the runway and the men finally relaxed, the engine caught fire. There were flames everywhere. I was ready to abandon ship—and had even made a lunge for the door—when the regular pilot suggested using the propeller to blow out the fire. That was not what was running through my mind, I can assure you. It worked and the emergency was over, but when those passengers deplaned, they kissed the ground. I think some of them looked for canoe rentals for the trip back. That day, those men learned powerful lessons about faith in God and the power of prayer.

Be Careful How You Pray

Of course you have to be extremely careful how you pray. I prayed for patience and got a husband. I prayed for wisdom and got five children. And I prayed for a sense of humor and got hips.

In all seriousness, you want to be real careful how you pray. I'm convinced that a lot of what I call prayer, God calls complaining. I not only tell Him the entire set of circumstances, I advise Him on how to resolve it, and also remind him of the time frame. More than once I thought to inform the Almighty, "If you can't handle this by Friday, I will handle it."

Now before your self-righteous Rita surfaces and proclaims "I'd never say that," keep in mind if you have ever had an alternate plan—in case God doesn't show up by Friday—you have already thought and done it. That hurts, I know. I am a pro at running ahead of His time frame. According to *my* time frame, He is *always* late. But on *His* timetable, He is always right on time. Never early, and never, ever late. More than once, I've learned that to run ahead of Him comes at a high price.

God's Work, Not Mine

I met a woman recently who has been in prison ministry for many years. Something she said pierced my heart, because I have found it to be so true. When she has an opportunity to share Christ's love for the inmates, she does not push for a hasty decision. "I don't make it easy for them," she said. "I don't encourage them to pray to receive Him into their lives immediately." When I asked her why, she said, "Because I want them to count the cost. Even though salvation is a free gift, it will cost them everything." Jesus said to count the cost before you ask Him into your life.

It really concerns me that today's churches feel the need to drive people to a quick decision. To me, that is a clear example of trying to force God to act on our timetable, and that scares me. I honestly believe that was why it took me a while to come to the Lord. I had caved in to pressure and prayed the sinners' prayer more than once, but my life never changed.

Realizing that bringing people to Christ is God's work and not mine has taken a lot of the stress out of sharing my faith with others. I want to be a witness for the Lord, but I have a terrible time getting on an elevator with complete strangers and asking, "How is it with your soul?" The Lord has delivered me from feeling I have to bow my head and ask every person I talk with to invite Jesus into their life. In a few instances where I was trying to "wax profound," the Lord has asked, "Are you going to do this, or am I?" It is so liberating to learn that our job is faithfulness, period. Sometimes we sow, sometimes we water, and sometimes we are there for the harvest. If we have the joy of sharing Christ and the listener feels compelled to accept Him into their lives, we have only been part of another's sowing and yet another's watering. Without question, it is God's harvest and we are only laborers in the field.

On the flip side, I have witnessed the "God squad" knock on the door of a victim, invite themselves in, sow and water for an hour, and then demand a decision—lest you die before they can get back. Good grief, God doesn't want folks pushed into the kingdom. Toward the end of the visit, I once whispered to the victim, "Pray—if you want us out of here tonight." Another time I wrote to a woman, apologizing for our rudeness in barging in when she said she was busy, and staying long after she asked us to leave. We not only didn't win her; we may have spun her out of reach altogether. I hate talking to people about the love of Jesus with a gun in their back, so I have resigned from the "God squad." I no longer believe I have to sow, water and harvest on the afternoon I meet you.

It seems that what was once a passion, has now become a profession. The truth of the matter is, if you reach out to others in the love of Christ, they will be drawn to you and to Him like a magnet. Hmmm. Wonder if that was His original plan. Could it be He wants to be involved in every aspect of our lives because we *need* help in every aspect? Several thousand years after the wilderness wanderings, Jesus said, "...apart from me you can do nothing" (John 15:5b NIV). Whether in everyday situations—or if our world is shaking on its very foundation—our response should always be to rely on His help.

One of the shakiest moments I ever had in an airplane came on the way home from a missions trip to Jamaica. Before we headed home, we filled out the paperwork notifying the United States we were en route, destination Miami. Completely unaware that the Jamaican authorities had failed to file the papers, we were a few miles off the Florida coast when I looked out the window and saw two Air Force jets overlapping our wings. I could not imagine what was going on. Those pilots were so close I could see the color of their eyes and the numbers on their helmets—and they could see the size of my dress. Way, way too close for me. I was flying co-pilot and whispered to the pilot, "What does this mean?"

"We are being intercepted," he whispered back. The words were no more out of his mouth when one jet fell back and the other pulled out in front of us and gave his jet full power. It shook our little plane so hard we began a dive toward the ocean. All you could see was water coming up fast. The pilot said, "If I try to pull it out, I'm afraid the wings will come off." The four of us in unison prayed just one word, "Jesus." Without a hand on the controls, our plane began to pull out and stabilize. We had dropped a total of 1500 feet. Though my world has been shaken many times since, I am now intensely aware that He can stabilize what I have lost control of.

My Shelter is Shaking

Several years ago, I hung up the phone, pieces of a conversation with my Father whirling in my mind like a blender...Mother...suspicious lumps in her breasts...scheduled for surgery tomorrow...be prepared for further surgery if malignant. Any one of those phrases hurl themselves into your mind like an enemy attack. They take your peace hostage and threaten your tomorrows. They dare you to look at all it could mean.

"We know you're busy," my Father had said. "There's no need to come until we know something for sure." It was so like him to shoulder the whole situation, yet somehow his voice lacked its usual strength and confidence. "We are praying and it will be fine."

"I am too," I said. "And of course I'll be there."

I was not ready to admit that the two strongest people in my life were vulnerable to attack. I have watched them weather storm after storm with rigid faith, and when gale force winds hit my life, I have run to them. How could my shelter shake?

After I hung up the phone, I put on my walking shoes to do my daily two miles. At times like this I need that sense of normalcy. As I closed the door behind me, I welcomed the quiet time ahead.

"Lord Jesus, please use this time to illuminate a portion of your word. Give me a promise that will be the lifeline Mother needs through this." Countless times Mother had pressed a paper with the exact scripture key into my hand—a verse that would call up a reservoir of faith and courage. Just once, I wanted to have that key for her. I waited, I listened and I walked. Nothing.

I quoted old stand-bys again. They were true, but they were like old letters—warm and comforting, but distant memories from the past. *What about now, today?* I needed to hear today.

I walked, waited, and listened some more. Still nothing. I refused to pray further, afraid the words I prayed would block the entrance to my mind and turn back the promise I desperately needed to hear. I neared home, feeling more empty than when I left. *I must be strong. Maybe I'm to go blindly by faith. Yet I so wanted to hear your voice today, Father.*

I walked into the house, ready to re-arrange my schedule, pack, and notify the family. There were so many things to do before the morning plane. My mind was sorting and filing my various responsibilities, trying to set things in order. As I worked, I began to whistle softly.

What is that tune? I had been vaguely aware of it all morning, but had pushed it aside for more pressing matters. *What is that tune?* I waited and I listened.

"Great is thy faithfulness"

Jesus is that you?

The words to that old hymn rolled through my mind. *All I have needed thy hand hast provided...*

That's it! That's your word, your promise to us, today's letter. I rushed to the phone. As the call clicked its way over the miles I whistled, "Great is thy faithfulness." "Mother," I said, "God has overshadowed this situation by speaking through the words in the song. All we need His hand will provide us."

"That *is* comforting," she agreed. "He has yet to fail us, and I'm sure He will accomplish His will through this. I know I am in His hands."

My brother, my daughter, and I planned to wait with Dad during the operation. We got in the elevator the next morning and bombarded him with questions. "Is she doing okay? How are you doing? Have they said anymore about the surgery?"

"She seems fine. I'm okay, and we have heard nothing new," he said. Dad seemed so fragile that morning. I knew the impact of all those "despicable" words we were hearing had taken their toll on him. I knew his shelter was shaking, and he, too, was wrestling for his peace and courage.

As we talked and prayed around Mother's bed, I think she almost enjoyed the little family reunion. They wheeled her down the hall, and we reminded her and ourselves, "Great is God's faithfulness."

We waited, drank coffee and asked each other, "How do people cope with crises like this without the comfort of Christ?"

Several hours later a voice said, "Good morning. The whole family is here, I see."

So this was her doctor. I had prayed all morning that he would see every problem area and would make wise decisions regarding them. Now I scrutinized his face like fine print. He had actually seen these intruders in mother's body and had marched against them. What did he know about my mother?

He spoke softly. "She did well through the surgery and is resting. We removed all the cysts, but we found malignant cells in one cyst from the right breast. We must remove the breast—tomorrow morning. She needs to be prepared for that when she wakes up. Are there any questions?"

"Are there any questions?" I repeated. "There are nothing but questions. She is seventy-eight. Is this absolutely necessary?"

"Yes, it is."

"Is there any possible way to treat it without removing the breast?"

"No, none at all. The only decision remaining is how radical the procedure must be."

I wanted to grab the doctor's arm and hold him still for an intense interrogation. At the same time, I wanted to push him away so I could pray. *What had happened? What do we tell Mother, or rather, how do we tell her? Where was the comfort of God's faithfulness now?* We looked at one another and at Dad, who was full of emotion, yet seemed empty, even hollow. We fought to keep control as we walked to her room.

"Is it all over?" Mother asked. "I feel good." She looked at each of us; we looked at each other.

My brother finally said, "Mother, they got them all, but there is a little more they need to do tomorrow. They are even now evaluating exactly what. They will remove the right breast, but there is the possibility it will be a modified procedure."

There. It was said, but now the awful weight had been shifted onto her. She seemed to deflate ever so little. "Well," she said, "we have prayed about it, and though I am not looking forward to it, we need to trust the Lord. He will see us through."

Shouldn't we be telling her this?

Eternity is the night before a surgery. Dad and I numbly went through all the motions, wondering what the days ahead would hold, and trying to keep our grip on "Great is thy faithfulness." Mother seemed somewhat refreshed the next morning. We didn't have much uninterrupted time with her as the nurses prepared her for the surgery. The nurses also helped us look forward to life beyond the operating room by asking Mother to choose her dinner menu. Her pastor was in the room when the anesthesiologist came in to reassure us of his role in this drama. We were all doing and saying the right things, yet I felt fragmented, as though parts of me sat in various places. *Pull yourself together.*

The phone rang. Since I was standing closest to it, I answered. "Hello? This is the doctor. Am I speaking to the daughter?" He continued, "I don't know exactly how to tell you this—"

My heart stopped. *What could it be?*

"I am in the lab now, and the pathologist informs me he cannot find the malignant cells he saw yesterday. It is most unusual."

My heart was racing now. I wanted to shout, but instead asked, "What does that mean? What will you do?"

"It means the malignancy is not apparent now." He seemed to be selecting each word carefully. "Though we will monitor your mother carefully in the next few months, I intend to send her home this morning."

I hung up the phone and shouted, "Mother, we are going out for breakfast!"

We did, but not before we filled that room with grateful praise for God's faithfulness. All we had needed His hand had provided. Years later, Mother has passed the "careful monitoring" of medicine—and we still praise.

When my shelter shakes today, I whistle, "Great is thy faithfulness" into the wind... *all I have needed, Thy hand hast provided...*

God promises to be faithful in every situation. Even though the children of Israel disobeyed and rebelled against Him, He was faithful and took care of them, even feeding them manna from heaven. When He takes you higher, farther, or into totally unknown territory, ask for His help. He will bring you down safely.

Chapter Thirteen

When He Says, "Climb and Maintain"
—Hit the Throttle

"OK, who lied?" the pilot asked suddenly.

The three other passengers and I looked at each other in confusion. The heavy-set gentleman next to me asked, "Why? What is the problem?"

"We were heavy on roll-out, and sluggish getting in the air," the pilot said. "On a more humid day, we could have had a serious problem."

Suddenly I knew what he was talking about—the weight of the airplane. Or rather, the passengers' weight. I knew I had hedged a bit, but certainly not enough to compromise the safety of the flight—or to confess.

I was quiet; so was everyone else.

Finally, the pilot said, "It is critical that you be straightforward with me about your weight when we are going to have a full load of passengers."

The seriousness of the situation suddenly became clear. If all the passengers—and there were only four of us—had hedged to the same degree I had, there was *at least* 100 pounds of undeclared weight on the plane. Our "hedging" almost got us wedged in the trees at the end of the runway.

The problem wasn't that the plane was carrying too much weight, the problem was how that weight was distributed. How you load an aircraft is critical to its performance, not only in the air, but on the ground as well. The balance of the load determines how much runway you need before you're airborne and the aircraft's safety and efficiency in the air. The key word is balance, and quite often you have to shift the load in such a way that you conform to the aircraft's load limits. It's a little like twisted panty hose; if they are not properly packed, they can cause you major discomfort and slow you down considerably. On the other hand, if they are packed appropriately, you hardly notice them.

Children and grandchildren have an uncanny ability to search out the kinks in your life and expose them to anyone who will listen. Nothing adjusts your sense of balance or causes you to shift the way you see the load any faster than they do. One of our younger grandchildren curled up in my lap not too awful long ago and said, "Nanie, I love you."

"I love you too, pumpkin."

"Nanie, what is that growing on your chin?"

"Well, listen Sugar, it is this *wonderful* gift God gives ladies called menopause. Now Nanie gets to grow a beard in an afternoon. I can teach the ladies' Sunday School class in the morning, and be a disciple in the cantata at night."

Since I am an educator, and we all want to learn, let me tell you that if you are *just* shaving your legs and under your arms, and *not* doing your chin, you are not mature.

"It's all in how you pack it," is another aviation term I have heard for years. I wonder if that relates to girdles, too? I once told a group of psychologists, "If one stitch in this girdle breaks, I'm launched." One gentleman piped up from the back of the room and said, "Don't worry, honey, when you come back down, we'll just re-pack you."

I now know that the real lesson of how you load an aircraft speaks to the balance necessary in my relationship with Christ. It is so easy to pack personal baggage into our life that He has warned would weigh us down and compromise our effectiveness and the safety of the trip. Hebrews 12:1 tells us in part, "Let us lay aside every weight and the sin that doth so easily beset us..."

I don't know about you, but I feel I have been encumbered long enough and am willing to shift and adjust what He wants shifted and adjusted. A few times He has told me, "Leave it on the runway. There will never be room for that in your life with me."

To lighten the load is to streamline the flight.

Tarzan, My Hero

We can learn a lot about balance from the experts. I love to sit around with other pilots and hear them *hanger flying*. That's when they tell stories about how they flew above or below the current danger, or how they circumnavigated the terror-filled odds thrown at them. My fascination with that kind of hero began a long time ago.

As a child growing up in Gainesville, Florida, Saturday was my favorite day. It was also my mother's favorite day, because she would take my brother and me to the movies, and drop us off there. That was back when you could drop kids off at the movies. You can't do that anymore. But she would drop us off, and we'd see a double feature, three cartoons, and a serial. Remember those days? Some of you do. You all are shaving your chins, too, I know.

Of all the movies I watched, my favorite ones were the Tarzan movies. I saw all of them, over and over again. In retrospect, I think maybe they only made one and changed the titles; I'm not sure. But I loved the Tarzan movies. I don't know why they had the impact they did on my life, other than that Tarzan lived a rather simple life. He lived in the jungle, in a tree house, on the river. What more could you want?

There was something else about Tarzan that just thrilled me. Tarzan was the champion of right, regardless of the risk. It simply didn't make any difference what the cause was, he was always on the cutting edge. If the bad guys came in to attack the jungle, or the plants, or the people, or the animals, Tarzan leapt to the forefront of the battle. The amazing thing I remember is he was always one step ahead of the bad guys. And he did it with weapons that appeared less sophisticated than the ones the bad guys had. Ah, it was wonderful.

He would save the people, the animals, the jungle, and then he would flee, with bullets whizzing past and the bad guys only an inch and a half from him. Just as they were about to catch him, he'd reach up into the jungle, grab a vine, swing down, and cut the water like a knife.

Did you know that when Tarzan hits the river, there's not a splash? It was wonderful. Then you would see him swimming underwater; oh, it was so amazing. Now if you are an amateur Tarzan fan, you look for Tarzan to surface sometime soon. Oh, no. Tarzan can hold his breath for a week and a half. You'd see bullets hitting the water and bouncing off, and he'd swim underneath it all until he was out of range. Then he'd surface and begin his bold strokes back toward home. You knew you were at the end of the movie, because Cheetah was on the bank clapping his paws. Oh, what strength. What endurance. What knowledge of the jungle. Finally, as he swam back, we'd start gathering up all our things. Just before the movie ended, we would take one last look, and way down on the far bank we would see a little movement. Something would slip off the bank and into the water with Tarzan. En masse, we would scream out a warning: "Gator!"

I worked with a girl in a real estate company in Atlanta, who was kind of like that. She would write to the soap operas and warn Doug that Julie was running around on him. I said, "I think he knows." She'd say, "He didn't

Friday." (Wouldn't it be scary to buy a house from somebody like that?)

Tarzan never heard our warning. Before he realized that gator was swimming with him, he would find himself in the midst of a life-and-death struggle with it.

Fear of Mediocrity

Let me tell you that mediocrity is the same way. You can be on the cutting edge of the cause. You can be on the forefront of the battle. You can actually have won some rather significant battles and even be making your bold strokes toward home, but if you're not careful, mediocrity will slip into the water and begin to swim with you. Take it from someone who knows. And you won't be able to hear the cries and the warnings around you, until you're in a life-and-death struggle with it.

You already know I'm afraid to fly, and I'm afraid of horses. Even the little mechanical horses in front of Kmart bother me a lot. I fear other things, too. I'm afraid you're going to find out what I weigh, or the size in my dress. I cut that out so Phil can't see it. "I'm still a 12 1/2, Darling." (Okay, so my right leg is a 12 1/2.) But I guess, if there's anything I truly fear, it is mediocrity.

Dr. Anthony Campolo talks about a trend that has begun to slip into the water and swim with us. And as I read about it, I realized it had slipped into the water and begun to swim with my family. He says, statistically, in larger families, the child learns to adjust to the system. However, in statistically smaller families, the family system adjusts to the child. Dangerous trend, really dangerous. I can't ever remember a time my mother said to me, "What do you want for supper?"

If we didn't want to eat supper, Mother would say, "We eat again in the morning." She didn't cook more than one meal for us. I don't know when this happened, but sometime between my children's childhood and my grandchildren, it dawned on me that I don't put onions in anything, because Christopher doesn't like onions, and I don't put carrots in anything, because Stephie doesn't like carrots, and I don't put cheese in anything because Kayla doesn't like cheese. I realized this little statistic had slipped in and begun to swim with my family. We were adjusting to the child. I'm not saying we shouldn't have programs that accommodate individual needs. But not to the exclusion of teaching our children and the next generation that life is a team sport, and you must play by the rules. So I gathered my grandchildren together and said, "Read Nanie's lips. Nanie is going to cook what Nanie and Papa want, and if you don't like it, we eat again in the morning."

"I'm Not a Morning Person"

When we lower the standard, and adjust the system too much to the individual, mediocrity slips in. I do a lot of management training, and six or seven years ago I was working with a large aerospace company. I was to help groom some people for management positions. As I talked with the man who hired me, I said, "Is there anything I can do to accommodate you in my presentation?"

"Absolutely," he said. "I want you to talk on ethics. I want you to talk on character. And I want you to talk about punctuality."

"Punctuality?" It seems to me, if you're supposed to be there at eight, you show up at eight.

"Yes, punctuality," he said. "Gaye, there are engineers—college-educated, graduate-degreed, engineers—that habitually come in 20 and 30 minutes late."

"You're kidding me."

"No, I'm not."

"Well, what do they say?"

He said, "To be honest with you, one of them actually said, 'I'm not a morning person.' So I want to know the appropriate response."

"The appropriate response is, 'you are not employed.' That simple."

God has called us to high places, but we can't go there weighted down with excess baggage we have gathered along the way—the baggage of laziness, jealousy, anger, mediocrity, unforgiveness, or bitterness. If you have traveled far with these things you know how they slow you down. They can get heavy enough to keep you from ever getting airborne. I have actually lugged my baggage into a church service, only to feed it and nurture it with a request for prayer. After all, if I could ask for prayer, that would give me the opportunity to unpack it and tell again how I had been mistreated. A few times I have parked these bags while I attended to other things, only to pick them up again later, dust them off and try to travel on. Whew, that will wear you out. It is Jesus who is supposed to tote the load. Give Him your excess baggage and watch yourself soar.

An Angel in Plain Clothes

I believe God once used an angel to put His finger on the mediocrity in my life. I needed to shift my thinking and get rid of some excess baggage that was weighing me down. I was in San Leandro, California, for two weeks of meetings in a church there. It was a rather small church, and I was staying at the home of the pastor and his wife.

On the first several nights, as I shared a little bit, I noticed a black gentleman in the back of the room. He was a large, well-dressed man, and for some reason I felt drawn to him. I wanted to talk to him, but could never get to him after the meetings. He would always slip out while I was talking to other people, and I wondered where he went.

The fourth night, he waited for me afterwards. When I got to him, he said, "You have a wonderful gift of teaching, but I will be so glad when you put your feet where your mouth is."

Then he turned and left.

That word dropped so deep down into my heart, it took me a long time before I could share it with anyone. Because he was right, you see. If you can check a book out of the library and read it, then you can teach it. That's all a consultant does. But you can't *impart* it, if you're not walking in it.

I believe God sent that man as an angel, because he never showed up again. God wanted to balance my life and he wanted me to understand that it wasn't the teaching He had called me to, it was to walk in His Word. I've done a lot of thinking about it and I tell it because it is a litmus test for me. It is important for me to never forget what that man said.

Our "Limbo" Society

Our definition towards life must be drawn from the scriptures. Hebrews 13:8 says, "Jesus Christ is the same, yesterday, today and forever. So do not be attracted by strange new ideas." Jesus Christ—and His word—are the only true standards we have today. It's scary when we deviate from them one iota.

Today we live in a "limbo society." You know the limbo. The goal of the limbo is to see how low you can dance without moving the stick or falling over. It seems to me that standards have sunk low enough. Almost anyone can win now, even in our school systems. I can tell you from firsthand experience that we have lowered standards in order to get students passing grades. When Madonna and Michael Jackson are perceived as winners, enough is enough.

I'm convinced in life's dance, it's time to push the stick higher and align it with God's standard. It is time to stretch to reach it, rather than slink beneath it.

Get rid of the excess baggage in your life, and surround yourself with people who make you reach for higher levels of truth, honesty, integrity and righteousness. Why? Because you cannot contribute to others more than you are. But the wonderful flip side of that is, you cannot give them less than you have.

Chapter Fourteen

**Clear New Pilots
for
Take-Off**

Two or three times a year, I substitute teach a very large Sunday School class at First Methodist in Ocala, Florida. I really enjoy it, because they are just the dearest group of people. On one occasion, I told the class some of my flying stories. At the break I overheard a man say to a retired Delta pilot, "Carl, I never knew things like that happened to pilots."

The pilot replied, "They don't, to *real* pilots."

There is always someone who has flown faster, higher, longer, and a greater distance than I have. They constitute a built-in mentor system, and lessons from these tutors provide amazing training—if we are willing to learn. Sadly, we often have to be forced to listen, or we wind up learning things the hard way. Like many of us, one of my first mentors was my Mother, who raised me according to the "old school." When I was coming up, the old school meant, "As long as you put your feet under my table, we do it my way."

Mother didn't labor under some of the misconceptions young mother's labor under today. She did not believe that if she sent me to school she would turn me off to academic values. As an educator, I know that in some cases, that's the mindset of parents today. She also did not labor under the misconception that if she took me to church every Sunday, she would turn me off to spiritual values. There were some things in our home that were not optional, and attending school and church were two of them.

But I had a lot of problems as a young woman. Thank goodness I only have room to talk about one of them. My most serious problem had to do with friends. I didn't have many friends, because I was over-possessive about my relationships. If you were my friend, I didn't want you to have any other friends, and I didn't want to have any other friends. So obviously, you didn't stay my friend for very long. If you didn't show up at school, I didn't know what to do before school, I didn't know what to do after school, and I couldn't eat lunch. (I'm over that now. Nowadays, if I showed up for a meeting, and nobody else did, I would eat my chicken and go home.)

Back when we called it breakfast, dinner, and supper, I came in around supper time one day and found my mother at the stove. She saw me crying and asked, "What's the problem?"

"Carolyn doesn't want to be my friend."

Mother had heard this several times before, and apparently, she had had enough. She dropped everything she was doing, and took me in by the supper table. I knew it was going to be a serious conversation because she put her hand under my chin and squeezed my cheeks together. Has your Mom ever gotten you like that? That's what's wrong with my teeth, so don't ask.

Then she did something very unlike my mother. While she held my chin with one hand, with the other she reached down into a big bowl of Jell-O and brought up a mound of it. She asked, "Do you see how much of that I can hold in an open hand?"

I said, "Yeth, ma'am."

She made a fist and squeezed the Jell-O back into the bowl. Then she said, "Do you see how little of it I can hold in a clenched fist? Only a stain. When will you learn to hold people loosely?"

I have never forgotten that lesson, and it has stood me in good stead. It has helped me in marriage and with my children and grandchildren. I have more friends today than I can count, because I have learned I can hold so much more of you if I hold you loosely.

Learning what to hold on to, and what to let go of, has been an eye-opener. Initially, it is hard to know the true value and worth of an item or, more importantly, a person. Can you conjure up in your mind the things and people you let slip through your life and now wish you could call back? I do, and it warns me to be careful.

That Cute Little Birdie

As I said earlier, my Aunt Irene did not have children. That meant she had china and crystal and Tiffany lamps in her home, because you can only do that if you don't have children. I was a teenage Mom and had a home in suburban Dade County, Florida. That means I had jelly glasses, fiberglass drapes in bright orange, rattan furniture with red flamingo's on it, and conch shell lamps.

One day, Aunt Irene gave me a print. It was a picture of a little birdie in this woodsy setting, all done in muted colors. It certainly did not go with my orange drapes or red flamingoes.

I thanked my Aunt profusely and stuffed the print under the cushions of my rattan couch. There it stayed, for years and years. Every once in a while I would drag it out and take another look. Nope, it still looked old-fashioned and didn't fit my decor, so I would put it back into storage under the cushions.

Then came the day we moved. I pulled out that print one more time. It still didn't match my decor, I still didn't particularly like it, and Aunt Irene would never remember she gave it to me. So I wadded it up and threw it away. I felt I had hung onto it for too long already.

Many years later it was my privilege to help take care of Aunt Irene before she died, and we became closer than ever during this time. Several times she said, "Now Honey, I put your name on these specific pieces, and your Mother's name on these over here, so that when I am gone it should be no problem to know what is yours." I assured her we were grateful, but that the real gift was her love for us. Her thoughtfulness, though, in making those choices did make it easier for us after she was gone.

One of the items she left me was an exquisite china cabinet. I brought it home and carefully cleared a place of prominence for it. One day as I was cleaning, I found an appraisal from 1958 taped under a drawer in the china cabinet. "Oh, this is neat," I thought. "I can at least determine what some of her things were worth in 1958." I unfolded the old appraisal, and by crackie, there was the china cabinet, the hand-carved chair, and the marble-top table. How exciting. Then I read, "Very rare Audobon print" and a description of the little birdie woodsy print I had thrown away. It was worth a great deal in 1958. I'm not sure I want to know what it would be worth today. Didn't fit my decor? Old fashioned? Muted colors that didn't blend with orange? If I had that print today, I would do my entire decor around it.

That was a painful lesson in "experience education." I had not measured the value of what I held in my hand, and had tossed it aside. I also realized the birdie print was a lesson I could now hand down. There comes a time when we not only learn from those ahead of us, but when we are also in a position to teach those who come after us.

I am a mother-in-law five times—but that is another whole book—and have lived long enough to have answers to some of the problems my children face today. They will ask, "How do you earn interest again, Mom?"

"One more time guys, it follows a little word called DEPOSIT." Some of them still struggle with that. I also know how to keep the wash from being dingy. You don't wash the whites in with the blue jeans. I have children who don't know that. According to Ann Landers, you can't tell them if they don't ask, and guess what? They don't ask.

Don't Throw It Out Before You Know Its True Value

The birdie incident brought one of my sons to mind. He has drifted a good long way from the Lord, and we don't hear a lot from him. I told my daughter, "I feel a need to write a letter to him, but I don't want to alienate him, and I don't want him never to speak to me again."

"Mother, how will you know if he doesn't speak to you? He's not speaking now."

She had a point, so several Christmases ago I wrote a 14-page letter to this son. I prayed over it and was very careful with it. I told him all the things I remember about him as a child. I told him I never hear the song, "And we sit by the fire, and we all perspire," that I don't think of him, because that's how he'd sing it. I told him what a wonderful Dad and husband he is, and how proud I am of him.

Then I told him there were some concerns on my heart, mainly that he's not addressing spiritual issues. I knew God had his hand on his life, and I wanted him to know it, too. Two weeks later he called. We talked around it a little bit, until finally he said, "I got your letter, Mother, and I let my wife read it. I told her that one of two things must have happened for you to write me a letter like this. One, you've found out some sort of medical news and are close to death, or you just had an accident a little while ago and maybe had a near-life experience."

I hated to interrupt and tell him they call it a near-death experience. I assured him I was not dying, but I almost wish I had let him think things were a little more serious than they are. Because you see, while he thought I might be desperately ill, my words carried more clout. Without thinking I said, "I'm not dying—that I know of—and in the accident, I did not have a near-life experience."

Then I said to my son, "I know my walk with Christ looks out-dated to you. I know you think you're more sophisticated than that, but I beg you, don't throw it out until you know it's true value. Be careful with it because that's what your Mom did.

"I considered a most valuable piece old-fashioned and out-dated and leaned on my personal opinion of beauty to define its value. After I learned the work of a master had been entrusted to me, my personal opinion of its worth vanished and it actually became quite beautiful in my eyes. The true value of anything is reflected by the master that created it. Be careful that you don't throw out anyone or anything before you know their true value. Reconsider your relationship with Christ. Do not discard Him lightly."

We all need mentors in our lives. The Lord gave us the apostle Paul as a mentor, an example. In the first chapter of Philippians, Paul said that even though he was sitting in jail, all of this had design and purpose. It was the work of God, not the enemy. Remember that God does not break out in a sweat when He sees your kids in trouble, or when He sees your marriage in trouble. He does not break out in a sweat when He sees your finances going down the tubes, or when he sees you gaining weight. God does not wring His hands when He sees your situation. Keep in mind, Paul is saying to us, that God is attempting to influence and resolve our situation. At the beginning of time, God looked at vast darkness, and said, "Let there be light." And light showed up.

He can look at the darkness in your life—or your child—and say, "Let there be light." I promise you it will show up. He said, "Let us make man," and a handful of dust leapt up and spun around in obedience, and stood there in male form, waiting on the breath of nobility. God breathed the breath of life into him. Oh, let me tell you, did he breathe. He breathed a nation.

We're not designed by the enemy and we're not defined by the enemy. God is in perfect control. Keep your eye on how God uses this, Paul says, keep an eye on it. It's a tapestry He's weaving. We're vessels on His wheel, and a work of His in progress. Paul measured his condition not by its present hardships, but by how effectively his circumstances would fall out for the furtherance of the gospel (Philippians 1:12).

Paul was a been-there-done-that pilot we can learn a lot from. He had blazed new trails through enormous difficulty. He constantly looked over his shoulder to mentor and encourage those coming after him, to help harness their fears and guide their way. Compassed about with so great a cloud of witnesses? Indeed, we are. Their voices still call to us, "Keep your eyes on how God will use even this."

June, The Avon Lady

Sometimes though, we don't know what God is doing, and we don't know how big the work is that God's doing. Thirty-something years ago, I had an Avon lady who lived only a few streets away. Her family had a terrible reputation, just terrible. June had teenage children who drank with them on the weekends, and a father who was godless. The police were at their house a lot, so they became the talk of the subdivision. Frankly, they were the kind of family everyone wished would move out of the neighborhood.

But because June was my Avon lady, she came to my house all the time. I still have Avon I bought from her. I tried so hard to witness to her, but she wasn't the type of person with whom you could just break out your Bible. Instead, as I was flipping through the catalog saying, "I'll take this lipstick in cotillion, and this blush in chartreuse..." I would say, "And you know what God did for me this week? I had a forty-six dollar light bill, and God..." and I would tell her whatever God had done for me that week. For months and months, June would come over and chain-smoke, and I would order Avon and tell her about Jesus. There was always a cloud over her, but it was not the Holy Spirit.

But you don't ever know how God will use your words. Revelation 12:11 says that we will defeat the enemy with the blood of the lamb and the word of our testimony. One day, just after she left my house, June called me. "Gaye, I want to get my daughter Jessica, and I want to come back to your house. I want you to tell Jessica some of the stories you've been telling me."

"Come ahead, June," I said. I hung up, grabbed my Bible and plugged in the coffee pot. I marked the Romans road—cause you know you can't win anybody without knowing the Romans road—sat down at the table, and there they were. Just as they got out of the car, I said, "Jesus, let them meet with You and not with me." Then they were knocking on my door.

While I served coffee, June introduced Jessica, and lit up a cigarette. "Tell Jessica how God healed your son."

I started talking really fast. "Well, you know, when my son was born, they said he'd never walk. He wore braces, and God spoke to me..." I told them about how God had shown me as a young, young, mother that He was going to take care of my child. As I got towards the end of that story, I reached for my Bible and said, "And there's something else I want to tell you—"

"Tell her how God paid your light bill," June interrupted.

I took a deep breath and said, "Well, I had this forty-six dollar light bill, and I went through my envelopes..." and then I started to say, "There's something else I want to tell you—"

"Tell Jessica about how God gave you those shoes. Tell her about that."

Each time I reached for my Bible, she interrupted. She would not let me get to the scripture. That was so frustrating for me because I'm one of those that grew up believing if you don't go to the cross by way of the "Romans road," you probably haven't gone.

In the middle of one of my stories, mother and daughter simultaneously covered their faces with their hands. I stopped talking. Wouldn't you?

June said, "Jessica."

Jessica answered, "Momma. Momma, can you see Him?"

There I was, craning my neck, and I couldn't see one thing. Nothing.

"I see Him," June said.

Jessica said, "Momma, His arms are out."

"I know. I know."

"Oh, Momma."

I was still squinting and craning my neck and wanted to say, "What else do you see?" Because I still couldn't see anything.

Pretty soon they took their hands down, and I don't know what to tell you except I knew they had met with Jesus. I knew they were born again. I said, "June, you met with Jesus."

"I know."

Jessica said, "Momma, I feel so different."

"I know. I do too," June said.

I sat there stunned, saying "Wonderful, wonderful."

They went home, and not twenty minutes later, June called back. "Gaye," she said, "How is it you get people healed, again?"

My first thought was, *Mature Christians can do it, but you're just a babe.* I didn't want her to be disappointed, though, so I asked, "Why?"

"The whole time we've been at your house, the hospital's been calling. My son collapsed on the football field. They have x-rayed him, and are getting ready to take him into surgery. He has a hole in his heart the size of a nickel. Now tell me again, before I leave to go down there, how do you get him healed?"

I thought, *I'll tell her to pray, but I'm calling the saints—the big guns—because she's just a little pistol. I'll call the big guns and we'll get him healed.* Don't you think that way sometimes?

I said, "June, pray. Just pray and ask God. We'll pray too. Call me when you get there. Put it in God's hands, June."

Later, June told me she hung up the phone, went into her bedroom and looked in the corner, and said, "Some call You Lord, some call You God, some call You Jesus. I don't really know what to call You, but Gaye said if I'll ask You, You'll heal him. Would You heal him? Amen."

I picked up the phone to call the big guns, and God said, "Don't touch it. I'm equal to the task." So I prayed and waited, and before long June called.

"Where are you?" I asked.

She said, "We're home. I told the doctors, 'Before you operate, I want you to x-ray him one more time, because he's healed.'"

"Oh, that's wonderful, June."

"They can't find the hole, so he's home. We're getting ready to eat. I'll talk to you later." Click.

Do you know, June got hold of that husband of hers—she's the kind who would say, "Get saved, or I'll leave"—and she and her daughter drug the rest of her kids into salvation.

But June's father fought it so hard. He fought it so hard June came to me just a few months later and said, "Gaye, I'm telling you, he is such a bad influence in our home. God has begun to bring His influence into our lives, that we can't have Dad here anymore. What do I do?"

"Pray about it."

So June prayed, "God if he doesn't come to You, take him."

Her father died within two weeks.

"Could you do his funeral?" June asked.

I wanted to say I was busy and had a hair appointment that day, but I couldn't. Because, you see, I'm the only gospel she knew at that point. So I agreed, reluctantly. I knew I would present the plan of salvation, but I also knew her father had been a godless man. I said to the funeral director, "This is going to be really short, okay?" He said, "We'll be close by."

I said, "No, if I were you, I'd stand right in the back, because this is going to be really short." All I knew to do was to say to that crowd, "God is a just God, and God knows the condition of our heart. I also know for a fact the gospel of Jesus Christ was presented to this brother, this man."

That happened back in the mid-sixties, but June and her husband, and all of her children, have since been on the mission field in Columbia. Once, when I told this story, a lady came up to me afterwards and said, "You know, it's really strange. I have a cousin I lost track of and she went on the mission field. One of her sons was killed in an airplane crash." When I asked what her cousin's name was, I found out it was June.

You don't ever know the shadow of influence you cast. As an educator, I'm always looking at those coming along behind us. How can God use me in their lives? I believe in order to touch the future, we have to encourage those coming behind us to reexamine our boundaries, to break our speeds, to test our limits. Before they're out of earshot, we must clear them for take-off to higher places. To trust the skies, to trust the wind, to trust their wings.

Learn from those who have gone before. Reach a hand back to those who come behind. Let them hear you say, "Fly high, fly proud. The voice of the controller will guide you through."

Chapter Fifteen

Are You a Real Pilot?

I have often been asked if I am a *real* pilot. I am never sure how to answer. Carl, the retired Delta pilot, would probably say "absolutely not." I know I can't leap to an immediate affirmative answer, but saying I am *semi-real* doesn't seem quite accurate either. I can fly a plane, and do take-offs and landings, but being a real pilot extends far beyond the ability to scream "roger" at every voice you hear over the radio. It even reaches beyond perfected take-offs and landings, navigational skills, and looking cool when you land. There is a lot to learn, and one of the true measures of a pilot is his ability to adhere to the rules when they don't seem to apply to him. There is also the recognition that in any life experience there are layers of learning and responsibility—and the learning is not complete until we can withstand the scrutiny of responsibility.

When one of my granddaughters was only a few years old, she spent a lot of time at Nanie's house. I have a metal-frame day bed and allowed her to eat in bed if she took all her trash to the kitchen. I even served her breakfast in bed almost every time she came over, and we had a wonderful time. I never had to clean up after her when she had snacked in bed. I was amazed that she was so meticulous at such a young age and bragged about it to everyone. When I complimented her on being so responsible about the candy wrappers and such, she would just beam.

Several years later I decided to have the carpet cleaned. As I moved the bed, the brass ball came off one of the posts and I gasped. *What is THAT?* The post was stuffed with candy wrappers, popcicle papers, popcicle sticks and heaven knows what else. The carpet under the bed also had a lovely fudgcicle brown stain on it.

I grabbed the phone and called my granddaughter. "What in the world have you done?"

"I thought if you didn't see them, they wouldn't bother you," she replied. We had a little talk about responsibility, and about Nanie's rules in Nanie's house. We discussed that when visiting here we adhere to my definition of clean and not hers.

I can't tell you the times I have bent the rules thinking, *Who does it hurt? Who will know? It looks good to me, and no one else does it that way.* The term rationalizing disobedience sounds brutal, but that is what it is. Once, as I asked the Lord to show me what stood in the way of my being all He wanted me to be, He said, "You want my will, your way. You want to fly by your rules."

Ouch! He couldn't have been more on target than that. Insisting on doing things our way leaves a great deal of debris and stain that, once uncovered, needs to be cleaned up. And uncover it He will, for part of His training in our lives is to bring us to His standard of righteousness, which is a far cry above our own. What we call clean, He calls filthy rags. What we call prayer, He often calls complaining. What we call making a request, He calls giving advice to the Almighty. It seems we not only feel the need to inform Him of our plight, but how it should be handled, and when. Makes you wonder how He ever handled anything before we came along, doesn't it? I have often flown through life with that attitude. It wasn't until I got into a hot spot that I learned the difference between what *I* had planned for me, and what *He* had planned for me.

Blooming' Hot

On the last night of an eight-week course I had been teaching at the college, the class gathered around my desk and presented me with a potted rose bush. Since it was winter, the rose bush was rather sad-looking, and completely barren of leaves. If not for the metal picture tag hanging on the thorny trunk, there would have been no way to tell what kind of rose bush it was. According to the picture, when it bloomed, it would be covered with beautiful yellow roses. A real promise of the growth to come.

A hard freeze was in the forecast, so when I brought it home, my husband suggested we set it on the hearth. The fire was out and only embers were left, so I knew it wouldn't freeze.

Imagine my surprise when I got up the next morning and found that barren rose bush covered with green shoots. Obviously the heat from the fireplace had forced it to begin to bud. I was amazed at the power it had to transform the bush overnight.

Then I began to think about the real impact of that experience. When we come to Christ we are barren and thorny, void of growth and extremely difficult to define. We look for all the world as though there will never be any bloom in our lives. I'm sure the reason we are allowed to wear the tag of "Christian" is so we can look at the picture He sets before us—the promise of what we shall be when He has brought us to maturity. I can tell you that when the cold season settles in over our lives, He has a way of placing us close to the heat until we begin to put on some growth of green. Faithful is the One who tills our lives.

When I think of all I have experienced in that little airplane of mine, I am reminded that being a pilot means new heights, new perspectives, new discipline, and new responsibilities. There are cloudless days with up-drafts that take you into layers of heaven you have never seen.

There are days of fog and weather that test your endurance and trust, and obscure your sense of who you are—and where you are. There are days that make you promise if He will get you down on the ground, you will never go up again. At other times, the Controller's voice is so strong it seems He is in the next seat and you want to whisper, "Did you see that?"

Being a pilot means occasions when the radio cuts out and all you hear is static, and all you feel is panic. *What should I do? What would the controller tell me to do? What was I taught to do?* It is terrifying and exhilarating; it is flying into dark clouds and flying out again. Being a pilot is having no idea where you are, and then recognizing landmarks again. It is feeling confident and capable—and completely uninformed. It is wondering whatever possessed you to test your wings—and not being able to wait until you can do it again.

Piloting encompasses risk and trust, fear and faith, full tanks and running on empty. It is cross-currents from hell, and balmy breezes from God's front porch. It is finding you can soar with the birds when you don't even have feathers, and playing hide and seek in the clouds and forgetting you were ever earthbound. Being a pilot is all that and volumes more. It is something you talk about and yet can't explain.

Am I a pilot? You betcha. Am I a real pilot? Yep, in training.

I am learning to hear the Controller's voice.

Are you?

For More Information, please contact:

Gaye Martin

PO Box 281
Summerfield, FL 34491

Phone: 352.288.2557

Email: P2GMartin@aol.com

Print books are available through Amazon, the Createspace estore and www.BusyWomenBigDreams.com. Gaye's book is also available in eBook format through your favorite online retailer.

www.ingramcontent.com/pod-product-compliance
Lightning Source LLC
Chambersburg PA
CBHW061438040426
42450CB00007B/1118